Precious PROMISES

A SYSTEMATIC DAILY DEVOTIONAL FOR CHRISTIANS

Based on the Authorised Version of the Bible

Editor and contributor
Rev James Cassells Kyle Paisley

Contributors
Rt Hon Dr Ian RK Paisley
Rev Noel Hughes
Rev Dynes Uprichard

⁘

Produced by
Vision Solutions NI
'Spreading the Gospel of our LORD Jesus Christ'

Precious Promises 1
© Copyright 2007 Vision Solutions NI

ISBN 978-0-9556218-0-2

Printed and published by
Vision Solutions NI
www.visionsolutionsni.co.uk
www.preciouspromisesbook.org

Genesis

Job

Matthew

⁜ **Dr Ian Paisley** has been preaching the Gospel of the LORD Jesus Christ for over sixty years. His knowledge of the Scriptures and his skilful abilities to both preach and teach are renowned in fundamentalist Christian circles across the world. The influence of Dr Paisley's ministry extends to countless tens of thousands who have listened to his sermons or read his books.

⁜ **Rev Kyle Paisley** has laboured as a minister of the Gospel in England at Oulton Broad Free Presbyterian Church since 1991. Today as an experienced pastor and preacher he continues to defend the inspiration of the Holy Scriptures and advocate personal and ecclesiastical separation for born-again believers. Rev Paisley has also spoken at several international Christian conferences.

⁜ **Rev Noel Hughes** began to preach the Gospel on the streets of Belfast as a teenager. Today he is minister of a growing congregation at Gardenstown Free Presbyterian Church in Aberdeenshire, Scotland. Rev Hughes has preached throughout the United Kingdom and also in the United States. During the early years of his ministry he also served the LORD for two years in South Australia.

⁜ **Rev Dynes Uprichard** is a native of Castlederg, county Tyrone. In his late teens he was converted to Christ and eventually called into the ministry. After serving the LORD for some years in Ulster he moved to Wales where he is minister of Pisgah Free Presbyterian Church in Swansea and the minister in charge of the Emmanuel Free Presbyterian Church in Llanelli.

In the Beginning God...

Mark the simplicity, authority and majesty with which the Divine revelation opens.
The Inspired writer does not set out to try to prove the Lord's existence, but without multiplying words affirms it unequivocally. In the original Hebrew, the strongest grammatical pause is under "God", calling us to give first attention to the Supreme Being.

What is this great God like?

First, He is All-Powerful
He "created the heavens and the earth" - the whole universe and everything in it (Genesis 2:1 - "Thus the heavens and earth were finished and all the host of them"; including the angels - Psalm 148:2-5; Job 38:7, cf V.4-7). Being created, they are limited, though in contrast to man they "excel in strength." However, He who made them is infinitely greater!

He is Eternal
The heavens and the earth could not exist without a beginning, but He who created them had no beginning. The Bible says, "He is before all things." John Bunyan was right when he said, "The first thing God created was time." Then God was also before time. He is "from everlasting to everlasting."

He is Tri-une
The Hebrew name used here is "Elohim". It is a plural of "Eloah" and is joined to a verb in the singular, showing Trinity acting in Unity (see also 1:26, 3:22, 20:13; Eccl.12:1). So God introduces Himself to us as the Tri-une God.

There is no other God but this God
As He is All-Powerful, reverence Him. As He is Eternal, trust in Him. "The eternal God is thy refuge, and underneath are the everlasting arms..." (Deut.33:27). As He is the only God, seek no other!

God's Word Supreme

Note that each day of the creation week began with God speaking.
"And God said" (V.3, 6, 9, 14, 20, 24). None of what followed would have happened apart from the Divine Word.

God also spoke during each day, naming things He had created.
Note the words "And God called" (V.5, 8, 10).

On the sixth day He spoke eight times (V.24-31).
He spoke the animals into existence, He spoke regarding His plan to create man, man's fruitfulness, man's food, what He forbad (2:16), a help for man (2:18), marriage - (Matt.19:5), and He spoke to name our first parents (Gen.5:2).

Days of creation also closed with God speaking.
The first day closed with Him naming the night, the second with Him naming the firmament, the fifth with Him blessing the animals.

All this shows that God's Word is supreme.
Nothing was accomplished without it and everything that was accomplished was excellent.

God's written Word is a word of power.
It reveals His mind and effects His purpose. As there is no creation without the spoken Word, there is no faith without the written Word - "Faith cometh by hearing and hearing by the Word of God."

Therefore, let us give it the proper place in our lives, believing it, and submitting to it.
Begin the day with the Bible and carry God's Word in your heart throughout the day. Have this attitude - "I will hear what God the Lord will speak."

Cosmos from Chaos - the Work of the First Day

The original creation must have been perfect.
Isaiah 45:18 says, "...the Lord that formed the earth... he created it not in vain (Hebrew 'tohu')..."

However, Genesis 1 verse 2 pictures the earth empty, a waste, dark and uninhabitable.
The original signifies a change from the condition of things in verse one. "Without form" is from the same Hebrew word Isaiah uses, 'tohu'; "was" in verse 2 signifies "became", and the same word is also rendered "came to pass" (Genesis 4:14, 22:1, 24:15). The cause, we are not told of here, but it is implied that "an enemy hath done this" (Matthew 13:28). In like manner man became a ruin (Psalm 14:1-3).

However, God did not allow this state of things to continue.
The Holy Spirit "moved" to prepare the world for change. God spoke, "Let there be light." Light was necessary for life and without it there could no vegetation and no food for God's creatures or for man.

Now, God's work on the first day of creation pictures His work in salvation.
Man's soul is in chaos until the Spirit works on him. In him there dwells no good thing (Romans 7:18). He is in darkness (Romans 1:21; I John 3:21; Psalm 82:5) and faces everlasting darkness (Matthew 25:35). But the Holy Spirit, by the Word of God, reveals the Saviour, and makes a man "a new creature" (2 Corinthians 5:17, John 3:7-8, 2 Corinthians 4:6).

If natural light is so precious, how much more Gospel light!
And God intends that it should flood the world! Christians take it everywhere, with the promise that God's Word will not return unto Him void (Isaiah 55:11).

The Changing Scenes of Life

In each day of creation, evening came before morning.
Without Divine Inspiration, Moses would have written, "And the morning and the evening…" But God's ways are not our ways.

Again, that which began in darkness was followed by darkness which ushered in a new day.

What is true in creation is true in many other ways. In all of life there are alternations of darkness and light.
Gloominess is followed by gladness (Psalm 112:4), sorrow by joy (Psalm 30:5), adversity by prosperity, and vice versa.

Life would not be life without such alternations, and they are necessary.
If life was all easy we would take God's goodness for granted. If it was all hard we would despair rather than trust in Him.

Providence permits alternations for good reasons.
Ecclesiastes 7:14 says: "In the day of prosperity be joyful, but in the day of adversity consider: God also hath set the one over against the other, to the end that man should find nothing after him."

In other words, we should not count upon things continuing as they are or reckon with absolute certainty regarding the future, but rather live in dependence on a gracious and all-wise God, and then we shall be ready for anything.

In all the changing scenes of life, commit your way to Him (Psalm 55:17).
Be encouraged too, that in Heaven there are no alternations, either physical or regarding circumstance. "There is no night there" (Revelation 21:25), "And God shall wipe away all tears from their eyes" (Revelation 7:17). Contrast this with the end of the Christ-rejecter (Jeremiah 13:16; Revelation 14:11).

Our Working God

From the beginning of the first day to the end of the sixth day, God's activity was unceasing. None of those days, nor any moment was wasted.

Moreover, the work of each day was varied.
Day One saw the creation of light, the dividing of it from the darkness, and the naming of both.

The work of Day Two was also a work of separation, but of "the waters from the waters" by "a firmament in the midst".

The work of Day Three was a "gathering" work (V.10) and a generating work - by God's Word "the earth brought forth grass" (V.12).

On Day Four God located the light to the firmament by making the heavenly bodies - the sun, moon and stars - setting them in place to "rule" and "divide". This division rendered permanent the separation and distinction made on the first day.

On Day Five, having prepared the earth for its inhabitants, God created mammals and birds. Land animals were created on Day Six, and finally, man.

God's creation work was finished, but His work in providence and grace is unceasing.

He guides His people daily (Psalm 32:8, Isaiah 58:11). He applies the benefits of a finished atonement to them (John 19:30, Romans 5:11). Jesus daily intercedes for them in Heaven (Hebrews 7:25).

Christian, show your appreciation for your working God by working for Him.
Follow the example of Christ, who said, "It behoves Me to work the works of Him that sent Me as long as the day is. The night shall come when no man may work" (John 9:4 - Wycliffe 1388).

Remembering Our Creation and Our Creator

Here our attention is turned to the origin of human life.

V.26 shows that God pre-planned the making of man.
There was a consultation within the Triune Godhead - "And God said, Let us make man..." It was vital that God should plan thoughtfully. The world was to have an intelligent occupant endowed with superior power and influence (V.26).

As Adam and Eve were not here by chance, neither are we.
There is a Divine blueprint for every life. Psalm 139:16: "In thy book all my members were written, which in continuance were fashioned, when as yet there was none of them."

Remember the power of God in the making of man (V.26).
He did exactly what He planned to do, but not apart from His word - "And God said..." Man has no existence apart from the word of God. True science confirms this. The DNA genetic code now reveals that all life forms are a result of a code of instructions.

Our creation by God teaches us many things.
Humility. How can we complain of or contend against our mighty Maker? No one has hardened himself against Him and prospered.

Happiness. Through Jesus Christ, though we are dust and ashes, we can commune with God (John 14:6, Genesis 18:28). We should make Him our first recourse in trouble and sickness.

Hope. This God is surely able to hear you and do for you great things (Ephesians 3:20).

Honour this God. Thank Him for the life He has given you and don't keep it to yourself. Commit yourself, body and soul, entirely to Him (1 Peter 4:19).

God's Masterpiece

Though man came after the beasts he did not evolve from them.
He is distinct. Both have a common Creator, but not a common nature. Man's physical makeup is different.

But he was different in another way - he was made "in the image of God."
The "image of God" is not a physical thing. The Bible says, "God is a Spirit." God the Son later took human form, but He did not have that body when He made the world.

The "image of God" is a spiritual thing.
Man is like God in that he is, essentially, a spirit (Genesis 2:7 - the soul was not generated with the body but was a separate creation), though God is an uncreated and un-derived Spirit.

His spiritual endowments include:
*   Freedom of will. Because he was made holy his will inclined to right.
*   Self-consciousness - the consciousness of a person. As somebody has said, "Not merely does thinking go on within me, but it is I that think."
*   Immortality. God lives from eternity because He never had a beginning. Man lives to eternity.
*   Conscience sets man apart from the animals who have no moral sense. An animal may be taught that it is not to do certain things but it is because these things are contrary to its master's wish not because they are wrong.

Man's being made in the image of God shows:
*   The sacredness of human life (Genesis 9:6); that it is impossible to worship God when you curse man (James 3:9).
*   Salvation renews the image of God and carries with it the promise of great glory. See Colossians 3:10, Romans 8:29, 2 Corinthians 3:18.

Bright Gems in Dark Mines

Job 1:1 "There was a man in the land of Uz ..."

The land of Uz is generally considered to have been located to the east of Canaan between the river Jordan and the river Euphrates, and north of the wilderness of Arabia. The name first occurs in Genesis 10:23 as that given to the great grandson of Noah through the line of Shem. It would seem the most probable conclusion that Job lived in this place during the patriarchal era.

The region itself was characterised by an ignorance of God. When Job's friends came from the nearby bordering tribes (2:11), they were reproved by the Lord for not speaking what was right concerning God (42:7). Although they were descendents of Noah and had the revelation of truth conveyed through him, their thinking and understanding had become greatly corrupted.

Job however worshipped God according to truth. Atonement by blood was central to his approach unto God. Each day he followed the divinely revealed pattern given to Adam, by offering a sacrifice unto God, (1:5). Job's salvation was grounded in the atoning work of the coming Redeemer (19:25).

He was also confident in and comforted by the sovereignty of God. In the time of affliction he worshipped saying "The Lord gave and the Lord hath taken away blessed be the name of the Lord" (1:21). His God was over all and in control of all things.

There was a man of God in the land of Uz. The brightest gems are found in the darkest mines. God's grace can produce and preserve the choicest saints in the worst of environments. Though your location may be like the land of Uz take courage believer, God has you there to shine for him as a light in a dark place.

A Perfect Man

Job 1:1 "There was a man in the land of Uz, whose name was Job; and that man was perfect and upright, and one that feared God, and eschewed evil."

Job's character is revealed in the opening verse. All four descriptions are like windows allowing us a privileged observation upon the work of grace in his heart. The first window opens to us his perfection, but what are we to understand by this term?

There is an *absolute* perfection of which nothing that is truly good is lacking. Only God, who created all things enjoys an all sufficient perfection in and of himself. He neither lacks nor requires anything that is good. No man can partake in this perfection.

There is however an *imputed* perfection which men can receive. Paul states of believers, that we are 'complete in Him', that is Christ. The perfect righteousness of Christ, whereby He fulfilled and satisfied every demand of divine law, is imputed to the believer's account covering all our imperfections and making us perfect, without fault before God. Job was perfect by way of imputation and so are all believers.

There is also a *comparative* perfection. It is written of Noah that he was perfect in his generations. Compared to the wickedness of the generation in which Noah lived, he was perfect. It is in this light that we must view Job. God said of him, "there is none like him in the earth" v8. Compared to those around him Job stood out by his godliness. He was not sinless but he lived a godly life by the grace and power of the Spirit of God. It is God's will that we be the same. Let us seek the grace which will cause the perfection of God in some measure to be reflected in us, in the midst of an imperfect world.

The Fear of the Lord

Job 1:1 "There was a man in the land of Uz, whose name was Job; and that man was perfect and upright, and one that feared God, and eschewed evil."

Job was a truly regenerate man. The evidence of his experience of the new birth was witnessed in his fear of God. He did not have a slavish dread, but a reverential fear that softened his heart and made him stand in awe of both the mercies and judgments of God.

Godly fear is the fruit of grace divinely planted in the heart, "I will put my fear in their hearts" saith the Lord, (Jeremiah. 32:40). The soil of man's heart is void of this grace until God regenerates the soul.

Job's fear of the Lord was manifested in his uprightness and eschewing of evil. Uprightness is conformity of life and inclination of heart to what is right. 'Eschewing evil', is the disinclination of heart and avoidance of what is wrong. The word translated 'eschew' is elsewhere rendered, 'to depart' (21:14), 'to withdraw' (33:17), and 'to remove away' (12:20). A God fearing heart will withdraw from the way of evil and walk in the straight path of righteousness.

Wherever the fear of the Lord is, the heart and life will always be enriched, for the fear of the Lord is His treasure, (Isaiah 33:6). Job was a rich man. God had deposited his treasure in his heart. True wealth is not based upon man's evaluation. The man whom God singled out from the whole earth was one who feared God. What God values is truly valuable. Count not your wealth by the quantity of earthly riches but by the possession of heaven's gold in your heart ~ the fear of the Lord.

Godliness in the Common Place!

Job 1:2-5 "And there were born unto him seven sons and three daughters ..."

Job's godliness was not the kind restricted to the cloisters of a secluded monastery. He walked with God and lived for God in the midst of his many taxing responsibilities.

He was a family man with ten children. Life in the Job home was by no stretch of the imagination a quiet or dull affair. He had upon his shoulders the burden of care for a large family.

He was also a business man and very successful in it. His flocks and herds were the largest of the region, and no doubt this brought endless pressures upon him. Animals to be fed and watered, pasture to be found, crops to be harvested, servants to be looked after and trading to be negotiated. Business and busy-ness was the order of each day.

In addition to these duties, he was engaged in the affairs of society. In chapter 29 he speaks of sitting in the gate, the ancient way of referring to the seat of council, or magistracy. He was very much respected and many appealed to him to help in social and civil matters.

In all of these various areas of life Job maintained his fellowship with God. For him communion with God was all important and the source of success and blessing for every other aspect of life. Job knew that his family, business and social life depended upon the blessing of God, therefore, he rose up early in the morning to seek the Lord (1:5).

Believer, avoid crowding God out of your life. Begin the day with God and bring the Lord with you throughout the day whatever you are involved in.

Satan the Accuser

Job 1:6-12 " and Satan came also ..."

Accusation is the master trade of the devil. In Job's case he questioned the sincerity of his motive, insinuating that he only feared God for personal gain. It was another attempt by the devil to usurp the prerogative belonging to God alone. God only can know and judge the heart.

It ought to come as no surprise that Satan attacks the character of the godly. He is inverately opposed to God and wherever he finds any reflection of godliness he will aim his fiery darts against it.

On this occasion God answered and silenced the devil's accusation by means of demonstration. He permitted the devil to afflict Job to prove that his heart was true and sincere towards the Lord. The Lord did not require to find out what was in Job's heart. He already knew, but to silence Satan and vindicate his own verdict of Job, He permitted the devil to lift his hand against him.

The work of Christ our great mediator has forever silenced the accusation of the devil against the righteous. When Christ ascended to the throne of God to present himself as our surety, the accuser of the brethren, which accused them before our God day and night was cast down. According to Rev 12:9-10 Satan is a down and out! His accusations cannot stand in the presence of the One who is the Lord our righteousness. Christ's obedience and blood answers the demands of the law, and silences the accusations of the devil.

Barred now from heaven the devil comes to torment believers with his insinuations and accusations. Should this be your affliction today keep in mind and rejoice in the knowledge that Christ intercedes for you and by the power of his grace in you will ultimately and eternally prove the devil wrong.

Prosperity and Adversity

Job 1:13-22 "And there was a day …"

It was a day when everything changed. The calm to storm, the light to darkness, the joy to sorrow, the prosperity to adversity. In one day Job's circumstances were turned upside down. The herds stolen, the servants slain, the flocks destroyed, his children killed. The contrast could not have been greater.

Life, like the pendulum of a clock can so quickly swing from times of prosperity to seasons of adversity. Both seasons bring with them their own peculiar temptations. In prosperity when all seems to be well the heart can become over indulged and neglect God. In adversity when everything seems against us the heart can become overwhelmed and curse God with bitter complaint.

The grace of God is more than sufficient to keep the heart faithful and submissive to God in either condition. Job did not forget God when all was bright and prosperous, nor did he curse God when the storm clouds gathered and darkened his sky. He fell down and worshipped, and in all this Job sinned not, nor charged God foolishly.

Job's exemplary response stemmed from a deep seated belief in the sovereign and all wise disposing of the Lord. He recognised his circumstances to be in the Lord's hand, his hand had given and his hand had taken away. He believed God had acted according to his unerring wisdom, for he did not charge God with acting foolishly.

Be content to leave your lot in God's hand knowing whatever He permits is wisely planned and will cause us one day to bless the hand that guided and the heart that planned it all.

Why God Permits Suffering

Job 2:1-10 "Again there was a day ..."

The events which had befallen Job brought great grief to his heart. But just when things seemed they could become no worse, they did. Satan was permitted to afflict Job with severe boils. His trouble was now compounded with bodily pain.

The intensity of Job's troubles raises the question why God allows suffering in the lives of his people? The Book of Job is designed to answer that question.

To **disprove the devil's accusation**. Suffering came again to Job because Satan said, 'touch his flesh and he will curse thee to thy face'. God permitted him to touch Job's flesh, but he did not curse God. The trial disproved the devil's slander. How much Job knew of the conversation between God and the devil, or that his trial was a refutation of the devil, we do not know, but the lesson for us surely is, that God permits our trials to refute the devil's lie. How many a prejudiced heart believing the devil's lie has been softened due to the patient endurance exhibited in the life of a tried believer!

To **deepen our experience of God**. Job testifies of the personal effect his suffering had. I have heard of thee by the hearing of the ear: but now mine eye seeth thee (42:5). His experience of God was deepened and brought to a new dimension because of what he endured. There is an experience of God that can only be obtained in the furnace of affliction.

To **display the grace of God**. The Lord magnified his grace in Job's life. When his friends came they saw the very great grief he was in. Every generation since observes in Job the sustaining and preserving grace of God. We marvel at the enormity of his trials. We marvel more so at the abundant, abounding and amazing grace that brought him through.

The Miracle of the Virgin Birth

Matthew 1:18 "She was found with child of the Holy Ghost."

The virgin birth of Jesus Christ is one of the cardinal doctrines of the Christian faith. Those who deny it both in ecclesiastical and secular quarters, seek to eradicate the supernatural from Christianity and debase it to the level of natural religion. The power of God can be seen throughout Christ's life, death and resurrection. Remember, "With God nothing shall be impossible" Luke 1v37.

The virgin birth was prophesied in the Holy Scriptures

The first promise of the supernatural birth of Christ was announced to Satan after man's fall (Genesis 3v15). The seed of the woman would triumph over him, not any from the sinful seed of man. The Lord prophesied that he would do a new thing, something unheard of before (Jeremiah 31v22). A woman would bear a child without any relationship to a man.

Isaiah prophesied that a virgin would bare a son who would be called Emmanuel (Isaiah 7v14). On seven occasions this word occurs in the Old Testament and on every occasion the word 'almah' means 'an unmarried woman'. Modernists should not ignore the sure evidence. The Lord was truly born of the seed of woman (Galatians 4v4). What a great mystery.

The virgin birth was possible by the Holy Spirit

Gabriel announced to Mary that she would be honoured among women by being the mother of the promised Messiah (Luke 1v28,30-33). Mary wondered how this could happen, as she knew no man. The power of God would do this miracle (Luke 1v35). The Holy Spirit, by his gentle operation took deity and humanity and fused them together and formed them, so that when Jesus came forth it was as the God-Man.

Just Joseph

Matthew1:19 "Joseph her husband, being a just man."

There are two Joseph's associated with the Saviours life. The first appeared at the time of his birth and childhood in Nazareth, the other at his death (Matthew 27v57). It is the first of these Joseph's that we want to consider.

Joseph was a just man

Micah the prophet declared a duty that God's own people must perform daily. They are to do justly (Micah 6v8), which implies that they live right with all men. This can be achieved because God works in every saint by the power of the Holy Ghost (Philippians 2v13). This divine strength within enables the Christian to live a blameless and harmless life in this world (Philippians 2v15).

Joseph was careful in every action to do the right thing. He obeyed the decree from Rome and paid his taxes to Caesar (Luke 2v1-3). Our guideline must always be to render unto Caesar the things that are Caesars. A refusal here will only bring the Lord's name into dishonour and destroy our integrity before men.

Joseph also refused to publicly shame Mary when he thought she had been unfaithful to their engagement vows. He had decided to break off the betrothal in private (Matthew 1v19) and spare her public humiliation. He dealt justly with her.

Joseph was just before God

God is able to raise up a band of justified men in a wicked place, Joseph lived during the reign of Herod the Great, who was renowned for his wickedness, yet Joseph was a just man who feared God. A man is justified before God by faith in Christ (Romans 1v17). All who seek mercy from the Lord are justified (Luke 18v13).

The Name Above all Others

Matthew 1:21 "And thou shalt call his name Jesus."

There are just over two hundred names given to God's Son in the Bible, which reveal his character and the great work he accomplished for his people. At Christ's incarnation there were distinct names given to him. One such name was 'Jesus', which was a common name among the Jewish people and signified their longing for the promised deliverer.

The significance of that name

Jesus means 'Saviour' and the Hebrew equivalent *'Joshua'* means 'Jehovah the Saviour'. It declared the great purpose of his coming, which was to save sinners (Luke 19v10). He saves from sin's penalty, which is death (Romans 6v23). He saves from sin's power over man and sets the prisoner free. There is a day coming when men will be saved from the presence of sin itself, when they enter Heaven.

He is able to deliver from sin as he has graciously given himself as a sacrifice for sin (2 Corinthians 5v21). As the Lamb of God he became our substitute and at Calvary finished the work of man's redemption. Salvation is freely offered to us without money or price (Isaiah 55v1). There is salvation in no other name (Acts 4v12).

The succour of that name

Jesus occurs 600 times in the four gospels. It is the most comforting of all names. Charles Hadden Spurgeon said, "This blessed name is the beginning of hope and the end of despair". When it was uttered in Joseph's ear it made his sleep peaceful (Matthew 1v20), and it dispelled all the shepherds fears (Luke 2v10).

This wonderful name is sweeter than honey, and is ointment poured on sinner's wounds (Song of Solomon 1v3). Can you say that he is your Saviour? (Luke 1v47).

God Our Companion

Matthew 1:23 "And they shall call his name Emmanuel, which being interpreted is, God with us."

Isaiah has been called the evangelical prophet as his prophecy abounds with reference to the person and work of Jesus Christ. King Ahaz received a sign that a virgin would conceive and bring forth a son called Emmanuel (Isaiah 7v14).

He is a condescending companion
The name reveals that Jesus Christ stooped so low when he was manifested in the flesh. He laid aside his glory and was made poor for our sakes (2 Corinthians 8v9). What humility of spirit he displayed. Peter the Great of Russia once left the palace and lived as a beggar in the village, only one man showed him kindness and gave him lodgings in his home. The next day Peter sent the royal carriage and brought the old man to the palace. It was then that the rest of the villagers wished that they had shown the king love and sympathy. Today the God-Man who has stood among men is yet unrecognised (John 1v26).

He is a constant companion
On occasions a friend might withdraw themselves from us but Jesus Christ is a friend that sticks close in every situation the believer faces. He is the refuge of the holy city (Psalm 46v5). He is the king in the midst of the camp (Numbers 23v21). He is with those who obey his great commission (Matthew 28v20). He has promised never to forsake his people (Hebrews 13v5). Charles Wesley rightly said, "Best of all God is with us".

He is a compassionate companion
Emmanuel is touched with our infirmities; his heart is moved when he sees men fainting (Matthew 9v36). He sympathises with you as a great High Priest (Hebrews 4v15). He cares for you (1 Peter 5v7).

Wise Men Seek Jesus

Matthew 2:1 "Behold, there came wise men from the east to Jerusalem."

Simeon's prophecy of the Christ child, was first fulfilled when the wise men from Persia came to worship the new born King. He, by the Spirit of God announced that Christ would be a light to lighten the Gentiles (Luke 2v32). An Old Testament prophecy uttered by Isaiah also came to pass, when Gentiles came to God's light and King's to the brightness of God's rising (Isaiah 60v3).

The learning of the wise men
As the Magi studied the movements of the stars, a new star appeared which they believed announced the birth of a King. Many in Jerusalem had the Law, Prophets and Psalms that announced the coming of the Messiah, yet when He appeared in the flesh they recognised Him not (John 1 v 26). How favoured by God we are to have the Holy Scriptures, that make us wise unto salvation.

The leading of the wise men
The Lord graciously made a star to shine in a dark place, so that men who were afar off from Christ might be guided to behold the Saviour of the World (Matthew 2v2).
The Gospel must shine into our hearts, so that we may behold the Lamb of God, who takes away the sins of His people.

The journey was a difficult one that was undertaken at personal cost to them. Only by striving do sinners enter in through the strait gate (Luke 13v24). The cost of self-denial must first be counted.

The looking of the wise men
Their enquiry in Jerusalem was "Where is he?" (Matthew 2v2). How earnest they were to find him. The Lord is found when He is sought for with all the heart, may you look unto him and be saved (Isaiah 45v22).

The Bread of Life

Matthew 2:5 "In Bethlehem of Judaea: for thus it is written by the prophet."

There were two places known as Bethlehem in the land of Israel. One was located in Zebulen (Joshua 19 v 15); the other, the birthplace of the Lord was to the south of Jerusalem. It was also known as 'Bethlehem Ephratah' (Genesis 35v19) as this region was fertile. Elsewhere it is called the City of David (Luke 2v11). Bethlehem means 'The house of Bread'. In (Ruth 1v6) Naomi heard that God had visited his people with bread after a great famine.

The sending of the bread
The Lord faithfully gave bread (manna) every morning to the Israelites in the wilderness as they journeyed toward Canaan (Psalm 78v19). The Lord Jesus was sent down from heaven as the true bread so that man might live through him (1 John 4v9). The Living Bread (Christ) is what natural mans needs to satisfy his spiritual hunger (John 6v35).

The sufficiency of the bread
The prodigal son realised that there was bread enough and to spare in the father's house for every servant and son (Luke 15v17). The bread sent from above is offered freely to any man (John 6v51).

The sweetness of the bread
As the manna was sweet to the taste (Exodus 16v31), so there is sweetness found in God's Son. May all taste and see that the Lord is good (Psalm 34 v 8).

The satisfaction of that bread
The saint will never hunger again; they lack nothing in Jesus Christ knowing happiness and peace with God (John 6v35).

Worshipping the Christ Child

Matthew 2:11 "And when they had opened their treasures, they presented unto him gifts."

It was an oriental custom that suitable gifts would be presented to a King, when one had an audience with him. Both the Moabites and Syrians brought gifts to David after he subdued them (2 Samuel 8 v2, 6). The Queen of Sheba brought King Solomon gold, precious stones and spices (1 Kings 10v2). The wise men too brought their gifts to King Jesus.

Their gifts were precious
Three gifts are mentioned - Gold, Frankincense and Myrrh (Matthew 2v11). King David would not offer to the Lord that which had cost him nothing (2 Samuel 24v24). Origen believed the gifts spoke of Christ's offices. The Gold was for a King, the Frankincense was for a Priest and the Myrrh was for a Prophet. Myrrh was used by the Jews to anoint dead bodies (John 19v39); it would have been of great value worth almost a years wages (John 12v3). Like the wise men may we give our best to Jesus.

Their gifts were preserved
Each gift was placed in a casket (Matthew 2v11) so it would be safe on the journey. Our gifts are only safe when they are deposited in Heaven (Matthew 6v20). All other treasures on earth perish because of the moth, rust and thief. (Matthew 6v19).

Their gifts were presented
When they came to the end of their journey, they laid their gifts at Jesus' feet and worshipped Him. (Matthew 2v2). Let us present ourselves to the Master, which is our reasonable service (Romans 12v1), so that we may have treasures to lay at his feet when he comes again (Matthew 25v20,22).

God's Finished Work

"Thus the heavens and the earth were finished and all the host of them."
The work of creation was full and orderly. "Host" stands for everything in the heavens - the planets etc (Deuteronomy 4:19); and the angels (Luke 2:13). It stands for everything in the earth, animate and inanimate. "Host" is used in relation to armies (Deuteronomy 23:9). Hence creation was perfectly arranged, well commanded, and ready to fulfil its Maker's purpose.

God finished His work in six 24 hour days.
This is clear from a number of things. First, the word "day" used in the previous chapter is qualified with a numeral. Second, it is limited by its boundaries "evening and morning." Third, the command to keep "the seventh day" in memory of God's finished work of creation (Exodus 20:9, 11) would be ridiculous if the word "day" stood for long ages.

God's finished work of creation typifies His work of revelation.
He has given us the completed Canon of Scripture. Other gifts of revelation have ceased (1 Corinthians 13:8) but the Bible is complete, full, orderly and sufficient to the purpose intended (John 20:30, 31, Revelation 22:18, 19; Ecclesiastes 3:14).

God's work of redemption is finished.
He ordered events in politics to this end (Luke 2:1-6). Galatians 4:4, 5 says : "When the fullness of the time was come, God sent forth His Son..." On the cross He bought us eternal salvation (John 19:30, Hebrews 9:12). He will apply all its benefits to believers and finish His work in them (Philippians 1:6).

Final thought :
Whatever you do for Him, finish it! (Exodus 39:32, 40:33; 1 Chronicles 28:20).

God's Rest Day, the Ordination of the Sabbath

It has been well said that the Sabbath is "as old as the creation."
God ended His creative activity, contemplated it with pleasure and approved it. Then He rested. There were no further creations, although He sustains His work providentially and His activities in grace continue.

The first Sabbath was not only God's testimony to His finished work (Exodus 20:8, 11), it also typifies His satisfaction with the finished work of redemption.
Christ made full atonement for us and satisfied Divine justice. His resurrection and exaltation were proof positive of His finished work. Now God "rests" in His love (Zephaniah 3:12).

God the Father rests.
He promised that He would by His pledge to glorify His Son (John 12:27, 28).

God the Son rests.
He knows His work is complete and He reigns victoriously (Romans 6:9, 1 Corinthians 15:25).

God the Spirit rests.
Through Him Christ offered Himself (Hebrews 9:14). Through Him Christ was raised (Romans 8:11). He is satisfied to apply the work of redemption to believers (Titus 3:5). God could rest at the end of the creation because there was no sin. His Gospel rest is because He has dealt with sin effectually.

We can enjoy the Gospel Sabbath by abandoning self-trust and resting in our great God and Saviour.
The Bible says, "For we which have believed do enter into rest... There remaineth therefore a rest to the people of God. For he that is entered into his rest, he also hath ceased from his own works, as God did from his" (Hebrews 4:3, 9, 10).

Our Rest Day, the Obligation of the Sabbath

In God's blessing the Sabbath Day and sanctifying it, He has given us an example and a command.
His resting does not imply weariness (Isaiah 40:28) but cessation from the activity He had been engaged in. So we are to take a day to rest from the week's labours - the day He has set aside. We need it because we do become faint and weary.

The Sabbath is binding.
If not, then all God's commandments are abrogated or the fourth is an exception. But they still stand. The Sabbath is now the first day, Sunday, because of Christ's resurrection. Mark 16:9: "Now when Jesus was risen early the first day of the week." The resurrected Christ met His disciples on the first day of the week, consecrating their gathering. (John 20:19).

There are spiritual reasons for observing the Sabbath.
Though the day has changed, the duties of the Sabbath are not changed. Christ, the Lord of the Sabbath teaches that we are obliged to do works of necessity on the Sabbath - Matthew 12:11 (remember that God continued to be active in sustaining His creation even after it was complete - Hebrews 1:3); we are to be at God's House on the Sabbath - (Mark 1:21), and give our attention to his Word (Luke 4:16).

To encourage the keeping of the day of rest God promises joy and success to His people.

Read Isaiah 56:2, Isaiah 58:13,14.

A Sabbath well spent brings a day of content
And strength for the toils of the morrow
But a Sabbath profaned, what ere may be gained
Is a certain forerunner of sorrow

The Generations of the Heavens and the Earth

V.4 marks the beginning of the second main section in Genesis.
"The generations of the heavens and the earth" signifies their "family history" i.e. their creation and further development.

Contrary to the critic, Genesis 2 is not a different account of creation from Genesis 1.
It is a re-affirmation of the fact that the universe in its entirety is from the hand of the Almighty. Compare V.4 with Genesis 1:1.

Genesis 2:4,5 confirm what Genesis 1;11, 12 say.
The plants had life "before they grew", because as had been previously stated, "God said, let the earth bring forth grass, and herb yielding seed after his kind, whose seed is in itself...and it was so."

All that was done, then, was entirely God's doing. He worked without the help of second causes.
There was "no man to till the ground" and the mist that "watered the whole face of the ground" was subsequent to the creation of the plants and herbs.

From this we learn:
- The world can do without man, but neither can do without God.
- This also emphasises the truth that God is distinct from His creation and His creatures, and is a powerful answer to pantheism on the one hand, and idolatry on the other. Nature is not God. Nor can God be likened to "corruptible man" (Romans 1:23).
- All materialistic notions of God must be rejected. If you are to worship Him then you must worship Him "in spirit and in truth" (John 4:24).

The First Man

The world was not only prepared for man, but man was prepared for the world.
The dust of the earth was fashioned into a perfect structure which was to be the home of his immortal soul. It also had, in its pristine condition, powers in such a high state of development that fitted it to be the servant of his immaterial part. It knew no fatigue, weakness, or disease.

Man's soul, however, was not generated with his body but subsequently in-breathed by God (V.7).
So man is something more than physical organisation and he is distinct from the animals. The origin of their "spirit" was coincident with that of their body and unlike man's, is not immortal (Genesis 1:21, 25; Ecclesiastes 3:21).

Man's soul was made "very good" - that is, holy as well as immortal, mentally and morally perfect.
So he has a knowledge of God and of his duty to Him, greater than fallen man can have. He had a disposition to right. His desires were after God. His delight was in God. Thus he was fit to rule for God.

Man is still responsible to God.
- To care for the world (Psalm 115:16).
- To care for his body by protecting it (Levitcus 19:28); to dedicate it to the glory of God (Romans 12:1, 1 Corinthians 6:13).
- To care for his soul by seeking pardon in Christ, and to do this before the dissolution of his body, after which there is no hope of salvation (Isaiah 55:6, Isaiah 49:8, Luke 16:24-26, 2 Corinthians 6:2).

Final thought - God's redeemed will be fitted to rule again (Revelation 5:10).

Man's First Home

For the man He had created, the All-Wise God had already prepared a home (V.8) - and what a home!
This garden is called elsewhere "the garden of God" (Ezekiel 28:13), and was famed for its beauty, provisions, fertility and locality.

"Eden" means "delight."
It was "pleasant to the sight." God would gratify man's natural senses there, which would inspire him to worship.

In Eden there was everything that was "good for food" (V.9).
Man's physical necessities were taken care of. God knew what was best for him in respect of his nourishment.

Eden's fertility is implied in V.10-14.
It was irrigated by four great rivers. "Pishon" means "full-flowing"; "Gihon" = "deep-flowing"; "Hiddekel" = "the darting", referring to its rapidity; "Euphrates" means "the sweet" and has to do with the taste of its waters.

The locality of Eden is noteworthy.
The region was rich in minerals (V.12).

God placed Adam in Eden to take care of it.
It needed cultivation, for the sake of continued provision (2 Thessalonians 3:10). It was to be guarded against intruders - the beasts of the field and that greater enemy (V.15, Genesis 3:1).

Man's first home is typical of the Christian's spiritual prosperity (Isaiah 58:11; John 7:38,39), but also of Heaven.
In its beauty and provision, its glory, wealth, activity, security (Revelation 2:7, 22:1, 21:10-21, 22:3, 21:27).

Let the hope of Heaven keep you from over-anxiety (Romans 8:24,25; John 14:1-3). Let your prayer be:

Do thou, Lord, midst pleasure and woe
For Heaven my spirit prepare
Then shortly I also shall know
And feel what it is to be there

A Match Made in Heaven

Genesis 2:18-25 - 'Everything about creation was "very good".

But God would not have made this pronouncement without His making a wife for Adam.

Note the fitness of the woman.
Among the animals there was not a fit companion for Adam, but in Eve He found the perfect partner. She was fitted for him in likeness of body, being "taken out of man." The word "woman" in the Hebrew is 'issha', the feminine of 'ish' = 'man.' She was fitted for him in likeness of soul, being made in the image of God too.

Note the fashioning of the woman.
She was the very last thing God made in creation.

The mystery of her fashioning. He put Adam to sleep. Adam slept before he sinned! (He who saw no corruption also slept - Psalm 16:10, Matthew 8:24).

The method of her fashioning. He did not form Eve from the ground, like Adam, but out of his side. There is no mention of him breathing a soul into her, because the writer only explains what was peculiar to Eve. Doubtless, the woman had a soul.

Note the favour of the woman.
God brought her to Adam as His special gift - this first marriage was a pattern for all (V.22, Matthew 19:4, 5).

This history speaks too of the Gospel.
True Christians owe their spiritual life to the fact that Christ died for them and because from His side flowed that precious blood which makes them one with Him. Their union is indissoluble and they owe Him all their love and loyalty (John 19:34,35; Romans 8:35; 1 John 4:19).

Cursing His Day

Job 3:1 "After this Job opened his mouth and cursed his day."

Until this point Job had exhibited godliness and grace of an exceptional decree in the immediate aftermath of his afflictions. He did not speak ill-advisedly but worshipped the Lord in the sovereignty of His will and providence. However, as the days passed and Job sat silent in his grief, his thoughts gradually descended into a slough of despondency.

In the first part of the chapter (1-19) he wishes he had not been born, and in the second part of the chapter (20-26) he wondered why he should be kept alive to suffer. He was greatly depressed in spirit. He could see no cause for his trouble. No possible good appeared to be the outcome of it. Nor could he see the way out of it. Hence, he speaks with bitterness of soul cursing the day of his birth, reasoning it would have been better had he not been born.

The aftermath of affliction is a perilous time! The mind can reason things it ought not to, and sink into depths of despair. It is a time when we must especially gird up the loins of our mind, put on the helmet of salvation, and set a double sentry with prayer and meditation of God's word. The word of the Lord alone will give us the answer we need.

But, following closely on the heels of trouble is the temptation to neglect the Bible and refrain from the ministry of the word of God. Yielding to it will only aggravate our trouble.

Job's meditation during the days of silence produced despondency. It was only after hearing the word of the Lord that he found deliverance (38:1). In seasons of affliction let us seek continually unto the word of his grace which will bear us up and bring us through.

Escapism - Wishful Thinking!

Job 3:11 "Why died I not from the womb?"

Job ventured upon an unsafe and unwise form of questioning. First, he asked why he had not died at birth, and second, he reasoned why he was continuing to live in the midst of his suffering, v 20.

In the first question Job's inquiry borders on the insinuation that God's way was unjust, unkind and unwise. Why did I not die at birth? Why have I been permitted to live? Under the dark cloud of his suffering Job forgot what Paul later reminded the Athenians of, that "in God we live, move and have our being." God gives us our being. God holds our soul in life. The Psalmist David wrote, "By thee have I been holden up from the womb: thou art he that took me out of my mother's bowels: my praise shall be continually of thee." (Psalm 71:6.)

The origin of our existence rests with God. He has given us life. He kept us alive in birth and sustains our life in this world. Therefore to question our existence in the manner Job did is to question the purpose, providence and power of God.

The inquiry proves to us that the very best of godly men can have a momentary lapse of faith saying things they later regret.

David's approach is the correct example for us to follow. He recognised the hand of God in the origin of his life and viewed his existence as a motive for praising God. David's birthday was taken up with thoughts of what God had wrought. Let us not curse the day of our birth but rather turn each anniversary of it into an occasion of reverent gratitude and worship to God for his power and mercy bestowed upon us when we first came into the world.

The Whys and Wherefores of Life

Job 3:20-23 "Wherefore is light given ..."

In this second inquiry Job moves away from the day of his birth to his present situation. He ponders in his mind why he should be kept alive to suffer. Wherefore is light given to him that is in misery? He had reached a point in his suffering where he thought it would be better to die than live in such a miserable plight.

Job was in the depths of despair yet we can detect a small degree of progression in his reasoning. It may not appear evident at first, but if we take the two questions together the difference will be noticed. In verse 11, his concentration is upon death, Why died I not from the womb? However, in verse 20, his focus is upon life. Wherefore is life given to the bitter in soul? He was viewing the opposite sides of the same truth. Death had been prevented at birth but life was prolonged in the midst of his affliction.

It is the latter consideration which reveals the beginning of recovery in Job's heart, for he acknowledges that life is a gift from God. Here was a glimmer of the faith that shone brightly when his trials first came. He replied to the news of the death of his sons, saying, "The Lord gave and the Lord hath taken away."

The remembrance of this truth would have furnished Job with the answer to his questions. The Lord had given life in birth and he had not yet taken it away in death. His life was prolonged in his suffering because the Lord had purposed it so.

When we find ourselves facing the whys and wherefores of life endeavour to submit quietly and confidently to the truth that God knows what is best and whatsoever he does is perfect.

Hedged In But Happy

Job 3:23 "a man... whom God has hedged in."

Job uses the same description the devil had used in accusing Job before God (1:10). The word *hedge* was employed by the devil and Job but with a vastly different implication in each case.

The devil implied that God had built 'an hedge' which prevented him getting at Job to really afflict him. Job however, viewed his hedge as a wall of suffering which he could not get out of. So the devil desired to get in and Job desired to get out but both were prevented by the hedge God had planted.

How thankful we should be that God plants different hedges about his people. Some hedges keep the devil from getting in, and others keep us from getting out. How many times have there been in our lives when the devil has been hindered in his desire against us because God put a hedge in the way? How many times have we been kept in the right way, in the path of God's will because 'an hedge' of affliction kept us from going astray?

Jonah was setting out on a course that would have taken him away from God and his service, until he ran into God's hedge. The Lord can make a hedge grow even in the midst of the sea!

Paul was pricked sorely by a thorn from the hedge God put in his way. That thorn punctured his pride and kept him on his knees in prayer. The great apostle discovered that God's hedge was designed only to give him a greater, deeper and sweeter experience of the sufficiency of the grace of Christ. Job discovered the same, and the hedge he initially complained about, he afterward praised God for. Let us do likewise.

A Bird's Eye View of Job

Eliphaz is the first of Job's three friends to speak. For seven days they had sat silent in the presence of Job. But now that Job has uttered the complaint of his soul the conversation between them begins. The book of Job is based upon these conversations. Chapter 4 to 14 contain the first round in which all three speak and Job answers them individually. The second round follows the same pattern from chapter 15 to 21, whilst the third round is recorded in chapter 22-31. After this Elihu gives his observation (chapters 32-37), and the narrative concludes in the last five chapters with the Lord's answer to Job.

The study of any book of the Bible will always be enhanced by first gaining an overview, or a bird's eye view of its general plan and content. The book of Job is no exception to this rule.

The book begins with the record of a sudden change of circumstances in the life of a man of God. In the midst of that adversity emerge the various opinions of Job's friends regarding the subject of suffering. Then at the end the Lord gives his own verdict on the matter.

The book of Job viewed in its entirety displays a very simple but highly significant message. Men have their opinions and ideas and they are all too ready to tell them. But the opinions of men are not a reliable foundation to rest upon in relation to this life and more importantly, the life to come. The word of God alone has the answer of truth. It is the sure foundation and all who build upon it will find the answer to life's perplexing questions.

What God Says Counts!

Great caution must be exercised when reading the comments of Job's friends. The key that unlocks the true interpretation and understanding of their speeches is found in the last chapter. The Lord having heard all that these men said to Job, declared unto them, "ye have not spoken of me the thing which is right, like my servant Job" (42:8). God's verdict sets us immediately on guard regarding their sayings.

It has been said that the most effective falsehood is that which has a little tint of truth in it. The speeches of Job's friends are best summarised in this way. They have a little tint of truth in them here and there, but there is much more that is erroneous.

Eliphaz is the first to reveal the error of his reasoning. As he considers the vast change in Job's life from prosperity to adversity, he begins by hinting that some sin must surely be the cause of this suffering. He put it in the form of a question in verse 7, "who ever perished being innocent?" He does not ask to gain information, instead he is insinuating that the presence of such great trouble in Job's life was surely caused by some great sin he had committed. His contention is not simply that sin is followed by suffering, but that sin and sin only is the cause of all suffering. He was espousing the belief that if you see a man in great affliction you will be justified in concluding that he has received that suffering because of sin in his life.

Job's experience proved otherwise. His sufferings were not on account of his sin. They were permitted in the providence of God. And being divinely permitted they disprove the error which Eliphaz advocated.

Fainting Fits

Job 4:3-5 "But now... thou faintest."

Faith in the greatest of saints is subject to eclipse. Job's shinning language of faith in chapter one and two was eclipsed by the reasoning of doubt and despair in chapter three. Eliphaz observed the change. He recalled what Job had been before his trial and how he had comforted and edified others. Now, on the receiving end of adversity his faith was shrouded and he suffered a fainting fit.

The best of God's people can faint in the day of adversity. Prayer is the only cure to revive the fainting heart. They that wait upon the Lord shall renew their strength... they shall walk and not faint, (Isaiah 40:31). Men ought always to prayer and not to faint, (Luke 18:1). The divine antidote for spiritual fainting is found in the place of prayer. Spiritual healthiness prospers when we maintain regular prayerfulness.

Eliphaz recognised Job's strengths and weaknesses. He was quick to highlight his weakness, but very slow to emulate his strengths. He commended Job for having strengthened the weak hands and knees of others and holding up him that was falling. But now that Job was in the same situation, now that he was weak and fainting spiritually, all Eliphaz can do is criticise and make insinuations. He did not attempt to strengthen Job's hands or try to hold him up from falling.

The descendants of Eliphaz are still to be found in large numbers today. They are quick to point out the weaknesses and faults of believers but they fail to exhibit their graces. Let us avoid their likeness and labour instead to have the testimony Job had as an encourager of the brethren, and an upholder of those who faint.

Jesus' Forerunner

Matthew 3:1 "In those days came John the Baptist preaching."

How greatly blessed John the Baptist was to be born into a God fearing home. Growing up with his parents Zacharias and Elisabeth he learnt what a privilege it was to serve the Lord. His father ministered as a priest before the Lord in the temple in Jerusalem. He also was taught how powerful true supplication is before the Lord. Zacharias had asked God for a son while his wife was barren and that prayer had been answered graciously when John was born.

The man John
John was sent by God as a forerunner to Christ, he sought to prepare the people's hearts for the Lord's coming (Luke 1v17).

May the Lord of the harvest send forth labourers today (Matthew 9v38). Will you volunteer for serving Him? On one occasion a king addressed a regiment of soldiers seeking volunteers for a dangerous mission. He asked them to step forward. Briefly he turned his back on them and then looked on the lines again, which were unbroken. He wondered why none had stepped forward. Quickly the reply came "We have all volunteered". - Will you?

John was spirit led (Luke 1v17)
The church does not require men of eloquence of speech or experience of service; rather it needs men endued with power from on High (Luke24v49). General Booth was greatly used of God, as there was a day when he died to self and the Lord had all there was of him.

As a young artist in Milan learnt that he needed not the brilliant artist's brush to be a great painter, but rather his spirit. May we be filled with the spirit of Christ.

John was a shining light (John 5v35)
Let us be radiant for God.

Preaching Repentance

Matthew 3:2 "Repent ye for the kingdom of heaven is at hand."

The true gospel of Christ when it was first preached by the prince of preachers in Galilee, commanded men to repent and believe the gospel (Mark 1v15). His forerunner heralded forth the same truth (Matthew 3v2), as did Paul who demanded repentance unto life and faith in Jesus Christ to be saved (Acts 20v21).

The essence of repentance
Repentance implies a change of mind, or a leaving of the sins we loved before and showing that we do in earnest grieve, by doing them no more. Like the prodigal son we must come to our senses and cease to live as madmen before God (Luke 15v17). Our whole course will then be altered just as the train that is diverted wrongly by the points man onto another track. It must apply its brakes and put its engine into reverse in order to return to the right track.

The essentiality of repentance
Without true repentance, men will perish in their sin (Luke 13v3). John the Baptist knew that divine judgment was approaching (Luke 3v7) and so he warned men to flee from the wrath to come. The axe had not yet fallen on the trees root, revealing still God's longsuffering with sinners' (2 Peter 3v9). Turn they must or burn forever (Ezekiel 18v30).

The evidence of repentance
Converted men will always bring forth fruits meet for repentance (Luke 3v8). Zacchaeus restored fourfold to those whom he had robbed (Luke 19v8). Truly he was a new creature in Christ.

Walking Humbly with God

Matthew 3:11 "... whose shoes I am not worthy to bear."

Moses was known as the meekest man in the earth (Numbers 12v3). John the Baptist walked humbly before the Lord, acknowledging that he was not worthy to perform even the task that the servant did when they unloosed the strap on their master's sandals (Luke 3v16). This is how every saint ought to live their life before their God, and remember like John Newton the wretched men we were, before God's wonderful grace saved us from sin.

Humility is required by Christ
There are three duties that the prophet Micah announced that the Lord requires in our daily lives. We are to walk justly (uprightly) before our fellow man and we are to show mercy (pity) to our neighbour. Our greatest duty is to walk humbly with our God. (Micah 6v8). This is how John the Baptist walked. During a time of popularity when multitudes throughout Judaea and Galilee came to hear him preach and the people had high expectations that he was the promised one (Luke 3v15), John refused to take any honour that was due to Christ. Immortal honours rest alone on Jesus' head.

We require lowliness of heart, for by nature we are proud creatures. May the Lord deliver us from being exalted above measure (2 Corinthians 12v7).

Humility is resembling Christ
When the Lord became man, he humbled (emptied) himself (Philippians 2v8). What riches he laid aside to become a servant of Jehovah and minister to others. He has set us an example to follow (John 13v15). Just as the wheat bows its head when it has ripened, so saints show spiritual maturity by exhibiting this virtue of humility.

Humility is rewarded by Christ
After humility there is honour. Christ was highly exalted to God's right hand after he glorified his father on the earth (Philippians 2v9).

The Symbol of the Spirit

Matthew 3:16 "He saw the Spirit of God descending like a dove."

Let's think for a moment today about the perfection of the Spirit.

The dove is clean in nature
The turtledove was regarded as a clean bird under the law (Leviticus 12v13-19). Dwelling within the believer the Spirit of God makes our bodies to be holy vessels. Christ calls his bride 'his dove, his undefiled' (Song of Solomon 6v9).

The dove is gentle
We are to be harmless as doves (Matthew 10v16). A bitter, contentious spirit is certainly not of God. One of the fruits of the Spirit is 'gentleness' (Galatians 5v22).

The dove's food
The dove is not compared to the raven that fed upon the flesh of the dead. Rather the dove returned to the ark so that Noah might satisfy her hunger. The Holy Spirit leads us to the Word of God, which is the finest of the wheat.

The dove's swiftness and strength
The dove was swift to do Noah's bidding and could fly for many hours because of her inner strength. As we wait on the Lord we renew our spiritual strength and are enabled to do our master's bidding swiftly in this life.

The dove's feathers
They appear beautiful when the suns rays fall on them (Psalm 68v13). When we commune with God, knowing the light of his countenance then our face shines like that of Moses (Exodus 34v29), and Christ's beauty is seen in us (Psalm 90v17).

The dove's fellowship
This bird flies in similar company (Isaiah 60v8). As the Lord sought fellowship with his disciples, may we love to be in the presence of the saints.

The Sweetness of the Spirit

Matthew 3:6 "He saw the Spirit of God descending like a dove."

There are many wonderful emblems of the Holy Spirit in the Bible. John the Baptist likened the anointing of the oil of gladness upon Jesus Christ, to the descent of a dove.

The productivity of the Spirit
When the comforter comes He produces life. At the beginning of creation, the Spirit of God moved upon the waters (literally he brooded over them as a dove - Genesis 1v2). Before His working there was darkness and no life. In regeneration dead souls are awakened by the life-giving ministry of the Holy Spirit (John 6v63).

When He descends he produces love among Christ's brethren (1 John 4v12). Saints especially seek to do good to all who are of the household of faith, proof that we are his disciples John 13v35.

The performance of the Spirit
Noah sent the dove forth from the ark once the judgement had ended (Genesis 8v8). Likewise our Father in heaven sent forth the blessed Holy Spirit after his Son had been judged for the sins of his people. If there had been no Calvary, there would not have been the blessing of Pentecost (Acts 2v2). May the comforter light on our lives so that we will accomplish our divine calling (Zechariah 4v6).

When the dove returned to the ark with an olive leaf, it announced a message of peace. Likewise the Lord was plucked out from the land of the living so that he might bring peace through his cross (Colossians 1v20).

Followers and Fishers

Matthew 4:19 "Follow me and I will make you fishers of men."

Passing by fishermen who were mending their nets on the shores of the Sea of Galilee, the Lord commanded them to leave their business and follow in His footsteps and he would make them to catch men alive. He is still calling his church to win souls today. The secret of winning men to Christ is learning to imitate Christ.

Follow Him by having a prayerful ministry
Every fisher of men is a man or woman of prayer. Luke reveals Christ's prayer life during those years of public ministry, both when He was baptised (3v21) and when He was transfigured (9v29). Jonathan Edward's well-known sermon 'Sinners in the hands of an angry God' was so effective as the previous evening Christians had earnestly prayed that the Lord would not pass them by.

Follow Him with a powerful ministry
Being baptised with water by John the Baptist, Jesus was then baptised with the Holy Ghost. This is what is needed in our ministries, a demonstration of God's power. When a miraculous draught of fishes were caught by the seven disciples on the Sea of Galilee, John recognised this happening as a manifestation of God's power; he acknowledged "it is the Lord" (John 21v7). Remember without Him ye can do nothing.

Follow Him with a passionate ministry
The Lord showed compassion toward the blind (Matthew 20v34) and to hardened sinners (Luke 19v41). Let us have a love for lost souls and a concern for the unconcerned.

Follow Him with a prudent ministry
"He that winneth souls is wise" (Proverbs 11v30). May we keep ourselves out of sight and use the right bait to catch men and women for Christ. Let us exalt the finished work of Christ on the cross. For this message has magnetic drawing power (John 12v32).

The Price of Discipleship

Matthew 4:22 " ... and they immediately left the ship and their father, and followed him."

A Christian is a follower of Jesus Christ. As sheep follow the voice of their shepherd, so every saint gladly follows every summons of their Good Shepherd (John 10v4).

Let us follow the Lord sacrificially

There was a cost
In order for James and John the sons of Zebedee to obey Christ's command; there was a cost involved. They left their nets behind them and their ship. The Lord calls men and women to serve Him faithfully in this generation and first we ought to realise that there is a cost (Matthew 19v29.) We may leave loved ones or a native land behind us, so that we might do his will for our life. Elisha counted the cost when he was called to succeed Elijah. He slew oxen and destroyed his plough so that he could not turn back to his former occupation. May we burn all our old bridges.

The sons of Zebedee forsook their previous means of support and stepped out with faith believing that the Lord would provide for all their needs (Matthew 6v33).

There was a constraint
The secret of following the Lord fully is the love of Christ taking hold of our hearts (2 Corinthians 5v14). Count Zinzendorf was quickened in Christian service by viewing Steinberg's painting depicting Christ's sufferings at Calvary. Henry Martyn went to India because he loved his master and would not go out free. May the Lord keep us near the cross.

Let us follow the Lord straight away
James and John did not question Christ's command but obeyed it immediately. May we not postpone any service to Him but go and work were He pleases (Matthew 20v 6-7.)

The Devil's Subtlety

What a scene we have here. The coming of Satan on to the world stage to seek, to kill and to destroy.
The Devil does not really introduce himself. He designs to retain his anonymity. He speaks not a single word of who he is.

Note how he always uses someone else to be his disguise and the slave of his workings.
Here he incarnated himself in the serpent. To betray Christ he incarnated himself in Judas Iscariot. He takes over others and uses them as slavish playthings in his hands.

In an un-fallen world no fears were felt.
What will happen again when Jesus comes was happening every day in the untainted earth. Isaiah 11:8: "And the sucking child shall play on the hole of the asp, and the weaned child shall put his hand on the cockatrice' den." So Eve was not afraid when the serpent spoke.

Eve was not aware of Satan incarnating himself in the serpent but she had knowledge that the serpent was more subtle than any beast of the field.
The speaking serpent was something which helped to entice Eve to her sin. The unusual-ity created an interest.

In the Devil's disguising himself we have an illustration of what his ministers do.
They present themselves as something they are not (2 Corinthians 11:13). But just as the words of the serpent showed the Devil's true character and aim, their words reveal what they are.

Therefore, let us not take as genuine everything that poses as Christianity. Remember that Jesus said, "For by thy words thou shalt be justified, and by thy words thou shalt be condemned" (Matthew 12:37).

The Devil's Policy

Let us learn that contrary to what mankind thinks, Satan's work is not in the grosser sins of the flesh but rather in the spiritual domain.
The grosser sins are the product of man's fallen heart (Matthew 15:18-19).

Satan's first move with Eve was to have her ask no questions about him but launch her into doubts about God and the veracity of His Holy Word.
He questions whether there were any trees whose fruit was forbidden. "Yea, hath God said?" He did not assert error. He did not contradict truth. But in questioning God's word he aimed at sapping the foundation of faith, obedience, morality, and established order.

Then he followed with a denial.
"Ye shall not surely die" (contrast Genesis 2:17).

Then he attacked God's goodness and promised Eve she would be a gainer by disobedience.
"For God doth know that in the day ye eat thereof, then your eyes shall be opened and ye shall be as gods, knowing good and evil." Note the baiting of the hook by the Devil with the same bait that caused his own damnation. Compare, "Ye shall be as gods" and "I will be like the Most High".

Beware of the Devil's policy.
Never countenance anything that undermines the veracity and authority of Divine revelation. Those who do will be prepared to believe a lie and to live as a law unto themselves. In the end, there is disappointment and death. The pleasures of sin are for a season (Hebrews 11:25); lawlessness is destructive of both the individual and society (2 Timothy 3:1-7), and the Bible says, "The wages of sin is death" (Romans 6:23).

The Fall and its Consequences

Eve listened to the suggestion of Satan and along with Adam disobeyed God. They fell from holiness by three things.
The lust of the flesh - "The woman saw that the tree was good for food". The lust of the eyes - "And pleasant to the eyes." The pride of life - "And a tree to be desired to make one wise" (see 1 John 2:16).

The consequences of the Fall were great.
There was *shame* (V.7 contrast Genesis 2:25). When Adam and Eve were without sin their view of things was pure. Now their knowledge received a new meaning. In every sinner the mind and conscience is defiled (Titus 1:15).

There was *vanity*. Their attempt to cover their nakedness is contrasted with God's way (V.21). All man's attempts to cover his sin are worthless (Proverbs 28:13).

There was *fear* (V.8). Fallen man is not on a quest for God! See Luke 15:13, John 3:20.

There was *hypocrisy*. Adam and Eve both passed the buck. Adam was the worst. He implied God was at fault (V.12,13).

So man, though created holy, was mutable.
Adam did not continue in holiness when he had sufficient strength. So what boast can man now make in respect of power and ability to obey God?

We all need an Almighty Saviour!
Christ is that Saviour. His righteousness is the perfect cover for our unrighteousness, and His blood purges the conscience, and makes us new creatures (2 Corinthians 5:21).

Scripture and our own hearts testify to how undeserving we are of this great mercy, and how worthy He is of our constant praise!

The Cursing of the Devil

Before the woman was told of the sorrow that she would occasion to herself as a result of sin, and before the ground was cursed for man's sake, God cursed the serpent.
Unlike the other curses, this was personal - "Thou art cursed." The serpent itself was cursed, which meant a "deterioration in its nature and a consignment to a lower position in the scale of being" (Joseph Exell). God punishes the vehicle of sin. The Devil himself was also cursed. His utter degradation was typified by the serpent's eating dust and going on his belly.

The cursing of the Devil was effected by the Christ of God.
He was crushed by the woman's seed (V.15). "Seed" is in the masculine singular and points to one - Genesis 21:12, Galatians 3:16. That One is Christ. He was to come into the world by a miracle birth. Bob Jones Junior comments in 'Fundamentals of Faith' - "Where in scientific literature is the seed spoken of as being in the woman? In the natural order of things, the seed is in the man; yet Moses, under Divine Inspiration, wrote of the promise of a virgin-born Redeemer. From this passage on through the Word of God we find this a dominant theme."

The crushing of the serpent was complete.
The bruising of the head means the striking at the vital part. By dying, Christ "destroyed him that had the power of death" (Hebrews 2:14, 15). Those who believe in Him triumph in Him, and can live victoriously daily. Romans 16:20: "And the God of peace shall bruise Satan under your feet shortly."

The First Promise

Hebrews 2:3 tells us that God's "so great salvation" was first preached by the Lord Himself.
This refers immediately to the history of the gospels and Christ's earthly ministry, but is applicable to what we read in Genesis 3. In Eden in the "cool of the day" He preached to them the first Gospel sermon, and spoke of Himself as the Deliverer. His sermon then was not unlike that to the two on the road to Emmaus, to whom He expounded in all the Scriptures "the things concerning Himself."

How sweet His words must have been to fallen man and woman.
Stripped of their glory, shaking with fear and crushed and cursed by sin, amidst their terrible night a light had sprung up. His word showed them that He remembered mercy "in the midst of wrath".

Thousands of years were to pass before His promise was fulfilled - but He fulfilled it! (Galatians 4:4, 5).
In that first promise there is the guarantee of everything that "pertains to life and godliness." We escape sin's corruption through the promises of God (2 Peter 1:4), but only in Christ are they pledged to us (2 Corinthians 1:20). They persuade us to embrace Him, set believers apart from worldlings and give them the sure hope of Heaven (Hebrews 11:13-16). Those who stand on them will endure to the end.

Standing on the promises I cannot fall
Listening every moment to the Spirit's call
Resting in my Saviour as my All in all
Standing on the promises of God

Sorrow - but not Without Hope

Our first parents had the promise of a Saviour but still had to face certain consequences for their sin.

Before the Fall Eve had the capacity to bear children without pain. After, God said, "I will greatly multiply thy sorrow and thy conception" (V.16).
The greatness of those pains is illustrative of the fear of the godless at God's intervention for His people (Psalm 48:6); grief caused by murder (Jeremiah 4:31); the howling of the impenitent at the judgment of God (Isaiah 13:6, 8; 1 Thessalonians 5:3).

God's word to Adam shows that through his disobedience the whole of nature was affected (V.17).
According to Romans 8:21, it is in "the bondage of corruption." See also Romans 8:22. One of the signs of a cursed nature was thorns (V.18). Christ wore the crown of thorns, signifying that He bore the curse of sin in our stead. That also guarantees a change in nature (Romans 8:21).

Adam was told that he would suffer as he exerted himself in his employment (before the Fall his work was all pleasure), and that he would die (V.19).
Death comes upon every sinner (Romans 5:12). God is true to His Word (Genesis 2:17, 5:5), and there is a death that never dies (Matthew 10:28).

But the dissolution of the body is not the end of the Christian's hope.
He goes to be with Christ, which is "far better", and he is promised a new body like Christ's (Philippians 3:21). With this hope Christians should comfort one another (1 Thessalonians 4:18).

Expelled but Expectant

God's knowledge of good and evil is perfect. He wouldn't be God if He did not know what good and evil were in their nature and in all their results. But He is at the same time absolutely set for righteousness.

Man's knowledge, however, was perverted by the Fall.
He knew what was right and wrong before he disobeyed, for God gave him His law. But he corrupted his own heart and disobedience followed. Contrast 1 John 1:5.

Had our first parents eaten of the Tree of Life in their fallen condition, neither they nor their succeeding generations would have had hope of salvation. So God set a guard to that tree.

The sword spoke of mercy as well as justice, showing that the way to Divine favour was only through the promised Messiah. Sacrifices later brought to the east of Eden preached the same (Genesis 4).

So though man was expelled by God, he was expectant.
Thomas Chalmers wrote : "The flaming sword at the east of Eden turns every way to keep man from the tree of life and under our Christian economy it turns every way but one - but that way is open and accessible to all. No man cometh unto the Father but by the Son, and He is the way and He also is the life. Out of that way no man shall ever meet salvation; in that way no man shall ever miss it.

"Stablish my feet O God therein; and through the open door of Christ's mediatorship may I find access to thee as my reconciled Father and Friend."

Strong Faith or Feeble Sense?

Job 5:1-7 "...and to which of the saints wilt thou turn."

Eliphaz continues with his insinuation that Job's trouble was caused by some great and particular sin in his life. When he states that affliction cometh not forth of the dust (5:6) he is merely saying that there is no smoke without fire. In his estimation there is always a cause to be found for trouble, and that cause is always due to sin in the life.

He was however mistaken regarding Job's experience. But in his own mind he was convinced of the validity of his opinion. Thus he gives the basis of his confidently held belief.

The first basis was his *personal observation* of life. Back in chapter 4:8 and now in verse 3 of this chapter he declares, I have seen. He appeals to his own observation and understanding of what happens in life. I have seen the wicked at first prosper but then crushed in the gate, all because of their sin. Therefore Job, your experience must fit into my observation and conclusion. Your trouble is due to your sin.

Eliphaz was leaning upon his own understanding. He believed only what he could see and understand. His religion was confined to the limitations of his own perception. He had not observed the communication between God and Satan, regarding Job. He was not a witness to the secret purpose enclosed within the infinite mind of the Most High God. Yet how forward he was to assert his verdict on Job.

The path of the believer in this life is traversed by faith, not by sight. There will be times when we shall not see clearly God's purpose. Let us not judge or confine the Lord by feeble sense. Let us commit our way to the One whose way is perfect and who will one day make all things plain.

The Only Foundation for Faith

Job 5:1-7 "Call now ..."

The second foundation Eliphaz rested his assumption upon was his claim of a *private oracle*. He informs Job of it in the previous chapter (v.12-21). He had a vision during the night season in which a spirit passed before him saying, Shall a mortal man be more just than God?

It is true that during the patriarchal era when as yet there was no written revelation, God communicated his will to the fathers by the prophets in various ways. However, Eliphaz is nowhere described as a prophet and furthermore the content and import of his vision are highly dubious. The inference of the vision is that a mere man would be considered unjust if he punished his servant without due cause. If some great sin were not the cause of the suffering God brought upon Job, then mortal man would be more just in his dealings than God.

The opening chapters of the book have already informed us that Job's sufferings were not a punishment for sin, but a demonstration of the preserving grace of God in a believer's life when he is buffeted by Satan. Therefore, the validity of Eliphaz's vision is called into question.

How privileged we are in this New Testament age to have the complete and all-sufficient revelation of truth now committed to writing. The written word of God is the more sure word of prophecy. Any claim of private oracles, visions, dreams and revelations must be tested by the plain teaching of God's Word. It is to the law and the testimony we must look and if they speak not according to this word it is because there is no light in them (Isaiah 8:20). The Bible alone is the foundation of faith and practice.

Popular Opinion or Divine Revelation?

Job 5:1-7 "Call now, if there be any that will answer thee ..."

The third court of appeal for Eliphaz's assumption was *popular opinion*. "Job, call now and see if any will agree with you. Inquire among the saints and you will discover that they all adhere to what I am saying. Can you find any among the upright whom God has dealt with as He has done so with you. Search Job, but you will find none. The common opinion of the saints is aligned with my contention."

Eliphaz reveals yet again the unreliability of his foundation. Popular opinion, even among the saints of God, is not a sure foundation to build upon. The people of God are exhorted to be of one mind and one mouth. Unity is described as a blessing to be cherished amongst the people of God and we ought to strive to maintain it. But we must be mindful that the important factor is not unity in and of itself. It is rather unity in the truth - a consensus that arises from the revealed truth of God. The unity Eliphaz alluded to amongst the saints was, if it really did exist, a unity based upon the error he was promoting.

There have been many times throughout history when the majority opinion prevailed, but it was not the right opinion. The most captivating example echoes from outside Pilate's judgement hall, when the crowd shouted, Crucify Him. The popular opinion was one which rejected the Son of God, but how wrong that opinion was!

We must not believe a doctrine or engage in any practice simply because the majority espouse it. The majority may be wrong! revealed truth must ever be our governing principle even if the majority reject it.

Presuming or Trusting?

Job 5:8-9 "I would seek unto God ..."

What we say we would do in times of trouble and what we actually do can be two very different things. How often have we heard or even spoken the words, "If I were you I would…" Eliphaz borrows this language, in essence saying, "Job, if I were in your situation, here is what I would do."

Eliphaz seems to soften his approach at this point. He has been exceedingly sharp in the preceding verses. Job had lost his sons and his substance and Eliphaz commented that such was the portion of the foolish (3-5). It was a harsh and insensitive statement, one that Job felt very deeply. Ye dig a pit for your friend, he replied (6:27). Words are very powerful, they can wound or heal, cast down or lift up, destroy or save.

In verse 8 Eliphaz gives advice that in itself was good. Right words however, can be said in the wrong way. There was an air of presumption in the way he spoke. He was presuming that he would act in this way if he were in Job's plight.

Presumption is most untrustworthy. Peter insisted how he would react if others forsook the Lord. Although all shall be offended yet will not I (Mark 14:29). He was sincere, and spoke with the greatest of intention. But he was presumptuous. In the space of a few short hours he was the first to deny the Lord.

Presumption is a counterfeit of true faith. It is self dependency, faith is God dependency. True faith renounces all confidence in self-ability and looks humbly to the Lord. It does not begin with self, but with God. If God will give me grace and mercy then will I be enabled to commit my cause unto Him in the day of my trouble.

Leaving the Choice with God

Job 6: 1-9 "Oh that I might have my request ..."

We come now to the response Job gave to Eliphaz. He answered by informing his friend he had already sought the Lord. Eliphaz had said to Job that if he were in the same plight he would seek unto God (5:8). His words contained a double presumption, he presumed on what he would do and at the same time presumed Job had not sought the Lord. Job however, had brought his complaint to the Lord and now he informed Eliphaz of what he had requested. He prayed that his life would be cut off.

We cannot help but feel for Job in his sorrow, but we cannot justify his prayer. It was evidently contrary to the will of God, for the Lord did not grant Job's desire. His life was not cut off at that time. God does not always give us what we desire, but He will give us according to His will, and that we know is always good, acceptable and perfect (Romans 12:2).

Prayer is a wonderful privilege and blessing for God's people. When we are overwhelmed with the burdens of life we can cast them all upon the Lord in prayer. We have access to the God of heaven through our Lord and Saviour Jesus Christ, and we are bidden to come boldly to the throne of grace that we may obtain mercy and find grace to help in time of need.

We can pray with the assurance God will answer. He may say No or Yes. Either way He has answered. The Lord did not grant Job's desire, but He still answered his prayer. Job later discovered that God's answer was best. Let us make much of prayer, but let us also submit the answer to the infinite wisdom and unfailing goodness of our God.

Pity the Man

Job 6:14 "To him that is afflicted pity should be shewed from his friend."

True friendship is proven in seasons of affliction. Fair weather friends are no friends at all. When the storm rages and the waves of trouble crash upon the vessel of life, then we discover the meaning of true friendship.

Job's troubles were aggravated by the censures of Eliphaz. He expected more from him, but instead his misery was increased. Eliphaz philosophised, and theorized as to the cause of the problem, when all the time what Job really needed was just some compassion and kindness. This would have served him more beneficially. A pitiful spirit seldom speaks but it listens often.

Job considered a compassionate heart to belong to the essence of true godliness. A person who withholds compassion from a friend in affliction forsakes the fear of the Almighty. He reveals an absence of the fear of the Lord.

John gives us the New Testament counterpart to this verse in his first letter, "But whoso hath this world's good, and seeth his brother have need, and shutteth up his bowels of compassion from him, how dwelleth the love of God in him?" (1 John 3:17) A sobering question indeed!

This compassion extends not only to other believers, but also to our enemies, "If thine enemy hunger feed him; if he thirst give him drink: for in so doing thou shalt heap coals of fire on his head" (Romans 13:20, consider also Matthew 5:43-48).

A pitiful spirit is a godly spirit, for the Lord is very pitiful and of tender mercy (James 5:11). The Lord is tender, gentle and merciful with us, and He wills that those who are His children should reflect His image in our treatment of others.

Miserable Comforters

Job 6:15-30 "My brethren have dealt deceitfully."

The latter part of this chapter contains Job's scathing reproof of his friends for failing him. When they came unto him at the beginning he had hoped to find some comfort from them, but as their conversation progressed it became clear they had merely come to insult him and charge him with hypocrisy.

Job charges them with acting deceitfully. They were like the bubbling brook, full of promise when the snow melted and the water flowed abundantly, but when the heat of summer arrived the brook dried up and the water vanished away, leaving the thirsty traveller disappointed. It is a charge and character we ought to avoid.

When our fellow believers are scorched by affliction let us endeavour to be like the waters of a refreshing stream unto them. The word of God is the fountainhead of that stream of consolation, for God is the God of all comfort. We can draw from the fountain of Scripture many a cup of cool water to refresh the weary pilgrim.

How much good Eliphaz and his companions could have done unto Job. Could they not have assured him of the everlasting love of God, which nothing can sever the believer from? Could they not have encouraged him with the glorious truth of the providence of God, in which He works all things together for good to them that love God and are the called according to his purpose? Could they not have enlarged upon the infinite wisdom of God, fortifying Job's mind with the knowledge that all things whilst unknown to us, are wisely planned by our heavenly Father? Perhaps their failure to do so only revealed their own ignorance of such truths.

The streams of earth will dry up but the unfailing reservoir of God's truth abounds with comfort and consolation for the tried believer.

God's Prophet Par Excellence

Matthew 5:2 "and He opened his mouth and taught them."

At the commencement of our Lord's public ministry He taught his disciples on a mountain in Galilee, (Matthew 4v23). His ministry concluded with instruction being given to his followers on Mount Olivet concerning his coming again (Matthew 24v3), and a little later on a mountain in Galilee he gave them a commission (28v20) and a word of companionship (28v20). He still desires every saint to learn of him, (Matthew 11v29).

Our Lord spoke with authority

When the Lord ended the Sermon on the Mount, his hearers asserted that he spoke with authority and did not speak as their Jewish scribes, (Matthew 7v29). Remember his word was that of a King, which is characterised with power (Ecclesiastes 8v4). In these last days, God has spoken to man through his son, may we hear him (Mark 9v7). Listen to him privately as Mary of Bethany did, (Luke10v39)

and as Cornelius did publicly, when his family gathered to hear God's word through Peter (Acts 10v33). May every ambassador of Christ open their mouth boldly and speak, as they ought to speak.

Our Lord spoke with the anointing

When the Lord was baptised by John, He received the oil of gladness above his fellows (Hebrews 1v9). The Holy Ghost, in the form of a dove lighted on Him (Matthew 3v16). God commands that every saint be filled with the Holy Spirit, (Ephesians 5v18). Learn to wait before the Lord to be endued with power from on high. Our enemies do not want us to speak anymore in His name, (Acts 4v18). Pray that the heavenly fire may come.

Our Lord spoke to the apostles

Every Christian has a responsibility to teach. Mothers train up your children in the way to go (Proverbs 22v6). Pastors feed your flocks (2 Timothy 2v2). May we be faithful where the Lord has placed us.

Good Grief

Matthew 5:4 "Blessed are they that mourn"

The second beatitude might appear at the first sight to be a contradiction. How can the mourner, who has been plunged into deep grief, be blessed? Our Lord uses a paradox to reveal that all who repent and mourn over their sins experience true blessedness.

What this mourning is not
Our Lord is not referring to a sensual mourning that is caused when someone does not receive what he or she lusts after. Ammon wept in this manner as Tamar had been refused to him (2 Samuel 13v4). Neither is it mourning because the Lord has punished our sin. Cain did not weep because he slew his brother Abel, but because he felt God had unfairly treated him (Hebrews 12v17). It is not the grief of a regretful soul in a lost eternity (Luke 16v28).

What this mourning is
It is a gospel mourning that occurs when the Holy Spirit reproves men of sin, righteousness and judgement to come and they cry unto God for mercy. Nothing is more precious before God than a penitent heart or a godly sorrow over sin. Let us also mourn over others sins. Paul was moved when he saw the city of Athens given wholly to idolatry (Acts 17v16). The Lord was moved with compassion toward Jerusalem and wept because of her impenitence (Luke 19v41).

What this Gospel mourning produces
One benefit is that we know the comfort of God's pardon (Psalm 32v1). We also know God's peace as we are reconciled to Him and have felt his kiss and embrace (Luke 32v1). What comfort we will receive in the life to come, then every tear shall be wiped away and we will be in His presence, where there is fullness of joy (Psalm 16v11).

Gospel Purity

Matthew 5:8 "Blessed are the pure in heart."

How happy are those who have been to that fountain drawn from Emmanuel's veins, such have been changed inwardly and evidence of this is seen in their outward conduct.

The place of purity
The Jews regarded the Pharisees as holy men because of their outward appearance of keeping all the duties of the law. Our Lord looked closer still, into their hearts (1 Samuel 16v7) and saw corruption within. The pharisaic spirit is still found in so called Christendom; there are individuals who honour God with their lips but their heart if far from Him (Matthew 15v8). Yet the Bride of Christ, the King's Daughter is all glorious within (Psalm 45v13).

The possibility of purity
God's will is that His people might be holy as He is holy. We can be sanctified daily through God's truth (Psalm 119v9). Every morning and evening be sure to bathe your life in those living refreshing waters.

The Holy Spirit purifies our hearts, He is compared to fire, which burns up all the dross (sin) and refines all it takes hold of. He is also likened to the wind (Acts 2v2) that drives away unsavoury odours whenever it blows. May the North wind and South wind blow on the garden of our heart so that the spices might flow out of it (Song of Solomon 4v16).

The prospect of the pure heart
We, like Job rejoice that we will see God face to face (Job 19 v 25-27). It will be worth it all when we see the Lord in all his beauty and glory.

Making Peace

Matthew 5:9 "Blessed are the peacemakers."

This attitude is, unfortunately, overlooked by many. It stresses the duty the apostle Paul taught to the Christians in the city of Rome, "If it be possible, as much as lieth in you, live peaceably with all men" (Romans 12v18).

Who these peacemakers are

There are many who are strife makers, who fail to heal estrangements between two parties, who do not stop quarrels among brethren or who do not reconcile those who are at enmity. Let us not widen the breach, intensify the bitterness or be seen to promote any hatred toward another brother. Let us rather be like Jesus and seek to be peacemakers. Remember, no one in Heaven delights in separating friends. Every saint must endeavour to still any troubled waters and strengthen the ties of friendship. Peace will never be promoted at the expense of truth and righteousness.

Gospel ministers are peacemakers as they declare through the Gospel of Jesus Christ that man, who is a rebel toward God, can become His friend through the forgiveness of their sins, by the marvellous grace of God. Every sinner needs to seek these conditions of peace (Luke 14v32).

Let us all as intercessors stand in the gap and turn away God's wrath upon a rebellious people, Moses sets this example as being a peacemaker (Exodus 32 v 10-14.)

Where to be a peacemaker

This role is vital in society were anti-semitism and sectarianism prevails. It is needed in the church too; so that brethren may be reconciled and God's blessing may be known there (Psalm 133v1-3).

The Salt of the Earth

Matthew 5:13 "Ye are the salt of the earth."

Our Lord Jesus used the common substance of salt, bought in the market place and used by housewives to preserve meat, to teach a vital spiritual truth. In the Sermon on the Mount, God's people are compared to salt for we are to have a preserving influence upon the ungodly in this world.

The salt's usefulness

Whenever salt is sprinkled it works silently there. Likewise the Christian by a holy, devout life toward God exerts a beneficial influence on all they come into contact with. Perhaps in the home of a godly woman there may be a husband who is yet unsaved, you may wonder how you are going to see them won to Christ? The Lord can speak to them through your quiet and gentle spirit, which will cause their heart to yield to God; (1 Peter 3 v1-2) "Likewise ye wives, be in subjection to your own husbands; that if any obey not the word, they also may without the word be won by the conversation (conduct) of the wives; while they behold your chaste conversation coupled with fear."

As we come into contact with other people, may our lives have a positive influence on them. Laban acknowledged that Jacob had been a blessing to him (Genesis 30v27). Equally the daily walk of Elisha who passed by her home (2 Kings 4v8) impressed the woman of Shunem. Welsh miners would not swear in the Welsh Revivalist Evan Roberts presence. He was a savour of life unto life.

The salt's uselessness

Salt loses its savour when it is exposed to the damp. Likewise it is possible for every believer to lose their cutting edge when they lose their power with God, this happens when we neglect the reading of the Word and prayer. Remember Lot's witness in Sodom? Because of his close association with the world his witness was ineffective. To his sons-in-law, he seemed as one who mocked (Genesis 19v14). If you have lost the power, ask yourself "where fell it?" (2 Kings 6v6) and retrace your steps, so that the Lord will heal your backslidings.

Shining for Jesus

Matthew 5:14 "Ye are the light of the world."

The beatitudes emphasise that every heavenly citizen has received numerous spiritual blessings in Jesus Christ. The Lord introduces two emblems of his people to reveal how they in turn become a blessing to this world (v13&14). Christians are to be lights in this world. The founder of the Waldensian Church, Peter Waldo recognised this role. Portrayed in the insignia of the church was the golden candlestick encircled with seven stars and the words "a light that shineth in darkness".

The symbol of the light
This symbol has always been used of God's people. Both Abraham's seed (Genesis 15v5) and the pastors of the Asian churches, (Revelation 1v20) were likened to stars. Like the star that appeared in the east, may we direct men from afar to come and worship Christ.

Our light must not be hidden through the fear of man, which can make us secret disciples of Jesus Christ (John 19v38). Christian, do not be ashamed to nail your colours to the mast. Speak boldly to others of the hope that lies within you (1 Peter 3v15).

The supply for the light
The light cannot shine of itself; it requires a daily supply of oil and the trimming of its wick. Likewise we become burning and shining lights in this world (John 5v39), by feeding continually on Jesus Christ and receiving his fullness.

The shining of the light
The light shines as a city on a hill, to help the weary traveller (Matthew 5v14), and as a candlestick in the home to bring blessing on our posterity (5v15). Like Andrew, be a personal worker and bring your loved ones to Christ (John 1v41). Many neglect their own vineyard and shine as the lighthouse, illuminating those afar off, but not those closest to them. May we be a blessing to all who are near to us.

The Law-Giver and the Law-Fulfiller

Matthew 5:17 "I am not come to destroy, but to fulfil."

The Lord clarified to His audience the purpose of His incarnation. His life, sufferings and death fulfilled God's Word regarding the promised Messiah.

He came to fulfil the prophecies of the law

All the patriarchs and the prophet testified of Him (John 5v39). His mediatorial work is announced under types and shadows. J.R. Miller said that this Old Testament tree is unlike any other fruit-bearing tree. In the springtime every fruit tree produces thousands of blossoms, but not all produce fruit. Yet there is not one prophecy on the Old Testament tree that is unfruitful. All is fulfilled in Christ, even to the minutest detail (the jot which is the smallest letter in the Hebrew alphabet and the tittle which is the smallest point) Matthew 5v18. As the artist does not destroy the first outline sketch in his finished work, so Christ does not destroy any Old Testament prophecy in accomplishing His great work.

He came to fulfil the precepts of the law

The Lord was born as a Jew under the obligations of the moral law (Galatians 4v4). He came and fulfilled the law and all righteousness. This is known as His active obedience. He honoured his earthly mother and Joseph. He sanctified the Sabbath day and He kept every rule regarding the holy feasts of Israel. He was accused of making the law null because His teaching contradicted that of the Pharisees. They rather made God's Word of no effect by their traditions. This perfect righteousness has been imputed to every saint by faith in Him alone .

May we learn, by His grace, to love the whole Word of God. No part is to be counted outdated, or to be discarded, or to be considered contrary to the Gospel.

Faithfulness

Exiled from Eden, our first parents entered on their life experience of labour and sorrow, and the human race began its onward course.

That Adam "knew" his wife signifies his love and faithfulness toward the woman God had made and brought to him in Paradise. It also shows that he recognised her nature and use within the marriage bond (cf Numbers 31:17, where "knowing" and "lying together" are used as one, and Romans 1:27 which speaks about "the natural use of the woman").

There is a moral union in marriage (the partners being one in heart) and a physical union. These mean that a man and his wife are virtually one being. Their being "one flesh" (Matthew 19:5) is a powerful argument against immorality (Ephesians 5:31, I Corinthians 6:16).

V.1 also illustrates the faithfulness of God to our first parents.

It was in keeping with His original purpose that they should "be fruitful and multiply" (Genesis 1:28) and He gave them the capacity to produce children. He had also said He would "multiply" the woman's conception (Genesis 3:16), and He did. Eve conceived twins. The words "she again bare" mean "she added to bear."

God's faithfulness and goodness in the gift of children is to be acknowledged. It also demands faithfulness from parents.

"Cain" means "acquisition". "Abel" means "vanity", and shows recognition of mortality. Children are a heritage from God, but they are weak and frail and parents ought to take good care of them. They owe this to God.

Religious Differences

The occupations of Cain and Abel were indirectly suggested by God in the command to till the ground (Genesis 3:19) and in the gifts of the coats of skin (Genesis 3:21).
But they do not indicate a difference in moral character. This is shown, rather, in their attitude to worship. As regards employment, there is great freedom of choice (Ecclesiastes 9:10, I Corinthians 7:20), but as regards approach to God, there is one way.

Now, Cain and Abel had a number of things in common in respect of religion.
They both believed in the existence of God. They both approached God at the set time (V.3: "In process of time" = "at the end of days", the end of the year, or the end of the week). They both brought an offering (V.3, 4). But here the similarities end. Abel's offering was accepted. Cain's was rejected (V.4, 5).

Abel brought the offering God required.
His parents had the Gospel preached to them in word (Hebrews 2:3, Genesis 3:15) and by type. The slaying of an innocent animal to cover their nakedness was a picture of Christ's coming to take away the sin of the world (John 1:29, Hebrews 10:19, 20). Adam and Eve, doubtless, taught their sons the Good News.

Abel's sacrifice showed his faith in the coming Saviour. Whereas Cain rejected this confidence and trusted in his own efforts.
Those who follow in his way will find themselves cast off by God (V.4, 11-13; John 12:48). Remember that you can only be accepted in Christ and that "without faith it is impossible to please God" (Hebrews 11:4, 6).

The First Murderer

Cain's reaction to God's rejection of his offering was to kill his brother.
He could not kill God, but he would kill the man God accepted.

Cain's act was deliberate.
He had opportunity to repent and believe and bring the right offering (V.7), but he would not heed the Lord. With malice aforethought he "rose up against Abel his brother and slew him."

Murder proves the corruption of the human heart (Mark 7:20-23).
A man can appear to be religious, but deep down in his heart cherish bitterness and vengeance. Remember, God looks on your heart (I Samuel 16:7).

The slaughter of Abel also shows that false religion is the greatest cause of blood-shedding. Millions since have been killed for it.
False religionists put Jesus to death. Today's global terrorism is the child of false religion.

But violence has no part in real Christianity. Not violent behaviour, or violent language.
As long as a man holds on to his hatred or cherishes violence he cannot be saved. I John 3:15 says, "No murderer hath eternal life abiding in him."

Of course, killing is lawful to save the lives of those who are suffering from violent aggression (Genesis 14:14, 17), or for national defence (Jesus never told the believing Centurion to leave the Roman army, Luke 7).
But the Bible says those who have "peace with God through our Lord Jesus Christ" (Romans 5:1) are to be "peacemakers" (Matthew 5:9). The Gospel is the greatest tool to reconcile men (Ephesians 2:14). However, when this is repudiated who can tell what will happen?

The First Martyr

Abel stands first in the roll of those who have died for their faith in the Redeemer.
Jesus showed this in His condemnation of the Scribes and Pharisees (Matthew 23:35).

His words reveal the character of a martyr, for He described Abel as "righteous."
That was by faith in the coming Saviour (Hebrews 11:4). God's having "respect" unto his offering (Genesis 4: meant the consuming of it by fire – as the original suggests. That offering spoke of Christ's dying in our place, apart from which we cannot be accepted with God (Hebrews 10:14).

So none can live or die a witness for Him who has not faith in the once-for-all sacrifice of the cross (1 Corinthians 13:3).

Jesus' words confirm the Old Testament account of Abel's cruel death, because he was speaking of the history of persecutors (Matthew 23:34).
Abel was a victim of fratricide, the guilt of which is emphasised by the recurrence of the words in Genesis 4 "his brother."

Christians too may be persecuted by those closest to them – brothers, parents, children, kinsfolk, friends (Matthew 10:21, Luke 21:16). They may not be killed as Abel, but there is always someone ready to murder their reputation. Still, for all you may suffer for Jesus' sake, He is worth it, and He gives this promise – "Great is your reward in Heaven" (Matthew 5:12).

The martyr's cry was for vengeance (Genesis 4:10).
Mercifully, God hears the cry of His Son's blood. He died, not as a martyr, but as the Saviour. So the penitent may be forgiven the foulest of crimes (Hebrews 12:24).

Divine Punishment

Cain was driven out from God's Presence, though he was more concerned about the consequence of his sin than the offence of it.
Thereafter he was to live a nomadic life.

His wanderings without God are a picture of the eternal punishment of the Christ-rejecter.
Jude V.13 says they are "wandering stars, to whom is reserved the blackness of darkness for ever." They are hidden from God's favour, because He will say to them, "Depart from me, ye cursed." It should be remembered that Cain's banishment from God's Presence was only part of his judgment. An everlasting "woe" is pronounced on him in Jude V.11. The punishment of sinners will not end (V.13).

It is a frightening thought that a man can be as good as damned before he dies.
Cain was beyond redemption. There was no hope of pardon for him and no hope of him changing. He lied and he attempted to defend himself (V.9). He did not pray for forgiveness. The Lord was not in his family life (there was no acknowledgement of His goodness in the gift of a son) or in his business (V.17). He never repented. He could not repent. He was like the rich man in Hell, who argued about the sufficiency of Scripture and God's way of dealing in mercy with sinners (Luke 16:28-30).

That sinners can be as good as damned before they die should make Christians urgent, thankful that they've been reconciled to God by the death of Son, before it was too late, and urgent about the business of evangelism.

Development and Degeneration

While he lived, Cain enjoyed temporal blessings.
He had a wife to share his sorrow (V.17). God gave him a family (V.17).

He sought satisfaction in earthly employments too (V.17).
His building a city shows his desire to counter his banishment and to secure himself against attack from those who would hate him when they learned of his crime. He also built in order for posterity.

Those who followed him developed agriculture and the arts (V.18-22).
So early man was highly intelligent, and not the kind of mindless animal some would have us believe.

However, despite his great advances his morals were still worsening.
Lamech corrupted marriage by being the first bigamist (V.19). He was also a hardened killer, taking advantage of one younger than himself, but thinking himself safe (V.23). He reasoned that if God showed mercy to Cain despite his killing his brother, and protected him, he would receive greater protection for a greater crime (V.24).

Today greater cities are being built, but they too are godless.
Technology is growing all the time, but man is becoming more self-sufficient. The relationship between a man and his wife is less revered than ever. Criminals are bolder and expectation of Divine intervention scorned.

So more than ever the message is to be sounded out, "Ye must be born again."
More than ever Christians need the sustaining grace of God to maintain a good testimony. The Bible says, "My grace is sufficient for thee," (2 Corinthians 12:9).

Consolation and Challenge

The birth of Seth was a wonderful compensation to Adam and Eve for the loss of Abel, and he was named accordingly.
"Seth" means "appointed."

God appoints many things for His people.
He has appointed them to faith. He has also appointed them to suffering (Philippians 1:29). Still they can "rejoice with joy unspeakable" for He has appointed them a kingdom (Luke 22:29).

There are many other encouragements to faith. For our first parents, it was the gift of a third son.
God made up their loss and provided a seed they expected to be godly, like Abel, but also to be the head of a family whose line would lead to the Messiah (Luke 3:38).

How good is God to His people in their losses!
Best of all, in Christ they have a feeling God (John 11:35, Hebrews 4:15).

Seth was a child of promise, but he had his challenges.
He lived in an age when men "began to call upon the name of the Lord" (V. This does not signify the institution of public worship, which had begun a long time before, but means that men appropriated God's name to themselves, thus taking the apostasy of Cain a step further.

Today God's elect are challenged by many antichrists (Matthew 24:5, 2 Thessalonians 2:4) who oppose the truth.
However, there is the promise of God's strength to resist (Psalm 18:32) and His pledge that He will keep us from falling (Jude V.24). This helps us to trust in Him and not to compromise.

God's Appointed Time (Part 1)

Job 7:1 "Is there not an appointed time to man upon earth?"

The answer to Job's question is full of *comfort*. The appointment is of God's making. Life is not a haphazard string of chance happenings. God has appointed our time. The day of our entrance into the world was ordained before the clock of time began to tick. Likewise, the day of our exodus from this world is divinely planned. How comforting to know that God is in control of all things. My times are in his hands. What I may consider to be dis-appointments are simply His-appointments.

The answer to this question is full of *caution*. Let us avoid with all diligence the snare of fatalism. That is the approach to life which says, "whatever will be will be, and therefore I will do nothing." The duration of our earthly existence is divinely appointed, but this does not mean we neglect the operation of secondary causes. We must not reason that since God has appointed our days we can forego taking food and drink, which are the means necessary for the continuation of life. God's decree embraces secondary causes also, and therefore impresses upon us our responsibility to attend to those means. The harvest is not appointed without the work of ploughing and sowing.

This principle is even more significant in the spiritual realm. The Lord has appointed his people unto eternal life, but not without their repentance and faith in the Lord Jesus Christ. But how will they repent and when will they believe? Only after hearing the gospel sounded forth by the church. Many were ordained to eternal life in Antioch (Acts 13:48), but they believed only after hearing the gospel from the lips of Paul. The harvest of souls will not be reaped without the sowing of the gospel seed by the church.

God's Appointed Time (Part 2)

Job7:1 "Is there not an appointed time to man upon earth?"

The answer to Job's enquiry is full of *challenge*. If our time is appointed then it is limited. We will not be here forever. Our days upon this earth had a beginning and they will have an end. How short that time is. It is a vapour that appears for a little time. In comparison to the great eternity of God our days are few.

But oh how quickly that little time passes! My days, states Job, are swifter than a weaver's shuttle, (v6). As the weaver threw the shuttle from side to side with swiftness, so the days of life quickly pass away. Queen Elizabeth I cried on her death bed, "Millions of money for an inch of time." Who can place a value upon time, yet how many are squandering it?

Christian, how little time you have to serve the Lord in this life! How little time to lay up treasure in heaven! How swiftly the opportunities pass to do something for the glory and honour of your glorious Saviour!

The word translated *appointed time*, occurs in Numbers 4:23, where it is rendered service. The service of the Levites in the tabernacle began at thirty and ended at fifty years of age. They had only twenty years of service. Our service for Christ is also limited. Let us endeavour to make our limited time, lasting service for Christ.

Perhaps you are not a Christian, how little time you have to prepare for eternity! We know not what a day may bring forth. If you have not yet made that preparation, tarry no longer. God says, *"Come now."* Christ says, *"Make haste."* The Spirit says, *"Now is the accepted time."* There is danger in putting off this matter of eternal salvation.

The Hope of Heaven: A Stimulus to Service

Job 7:1-11 "... as an hireling looketh for the reward of his work."

Job likens himself to the paid servant who works for his master looking for the end of the day when he shall receive his wage. His sore affliction had made him restless and weary, creating within a longing to escape the toil of this world. He knew his time was appointed in its duration and therefore he longed for its end.

Job was right in a measure. As believers we must guard against being too settled in this world. We are passing through to the heavenly kingdom, and we must ever regard ourselves as strangers and pilgrims upon this earth.

It is when we allow our hearts to become too attached to the world, and earthbound, that the Lord often in His mercy permits the trials of life. They have the effect of loosening the roots, and drawing the affections of our heart to Himself. You may be enduring a sore trial just now in your life, believer. Here is one reason, among others, why it may have been sent. The Lord does not permit His children to become too attached to this world.

Job however was not altogether right in his restlessness. There is a sense in which it is lawful for a Christian to look forward with anticipation of the joys of heaven. The danger comes when the desire to depart adversely affects our service upon the earth. Paul had a desire to depart and be with Christ, but he also recognised his Lord had a purpose for him remaining. To the Philippians he wrote, "nevertheless to abide in the flesh is more needful for you" (Phil 1:24).

Our expectation of heaven ought not to stifle, our service for the Lord on earth, it ought to stimulate and strengthen it all the more.

Job Defends His Innocence

Job 7:12-21 "Am I a sea , or a whale that thou settest a watch over me?"

From this part of the chapter Job begins to address an individual person, as evidenced by the word thou. There is a difference of interpretation as to the identity of the person. One opinion believes Job is speaking to the Lord, whilst the other considers Eliphaz to be the one addressed.

The passage appears to identify Eliphaz as the individual. In chapter 4:12-21 Eliphaz made reference to his vision, and now in verse 14 of this chapter Job responds saying, "thou scarest me with dreams and terrifiest me through visions."

This latter part of the passage is Job's complaint regarding his friends. They had aggravated his trouble and misery. Now he is saying to them, "if I am such a sinful and miserable man, and a man appointed unto death, why do you make so much of me? Why do you magnify me? Why do you not just overlook my sin, which you allege is the cause of my sorrow? What have I done against thee? Has my alleged sin been against you? He was in reality, not confessing sin but defending his innocence.

If we view the passage in this light, it will agree with the occasions when he pleads his innocence, 10:7; 23:11; 27:5-6. It is evident that Job's friends also interpreted his confession as a defence, Bildad 8:6, Zophar 11:4, Eliphaz 15:13-14, and Elihu 33:8-9. They did not consider him to be genuinely confessing sin, but defending himself from their charge that a grievous sin in his life was cause of his uncommon suffering.

Job's suffering was not due to one particular sin. He was exemplary in his uprightness, as the Lord himself had said. Job however was not without sin, and his peculiar trials would cause him to see that when he would do good evil was present with him.

Delayed Intervention – No Punishment!

Job 8:1-7 "if thou wert pure and upright; surely now he would awake for thee ..."

Bildad, the second of Job's friends stepped forth unto the stage at this point. He does so with a sense of urgency and necessity. He cannot tolerate Job's speech any longer and feels he must now challenge him.

What Bildad said would plainly indicate he did not believe Job had made a genuine confession of sin in the previous passage. In his mind, Job had not accepted the argument of Eliphaz that great suffering is always and only due to grievous sin in the life.

Bildad introduces another line of argument in his effort to convince Job. If you really were a pure and upright man then God would intervene to help you. You would not be in this state. God would come speedily to your side and make your habitation prosperous. But surely his lack of intervention reveals the hypocrisy of your heart.

Bildad had fallen into the snare so many become entangled in. They judge a man's standing before God by his outward circumstances. They reason like Eliphaz that adversity implies God's anger, and like Bildad, that prosperity indicates God's favour upon a man.

Scripture permits us to make no such assumption. Chastening is the sign of love, for whom the Lord loveth he chasteneth. Prosperity is no sign of a favourable standing in the sight of God, for God makes the sun to rise on the evil and the good. The righteous may be afflicted whilst the wicked flourish. The outward circumstances are not a certain sign of the inward condition of the heart.

Only the Lord can see and know the heart, therefore it is better to be reticent in judging a man's position, following Paul's exhortation to "judge nothing before the time, until the Lord come... who will make manifest the counsels of the heart" (1 Cor 4:5).

The Mystery of Providence and the Ground of Grace

Job 8: 1-7 "If thou wert pure ..."

Bildad's reproof of Job failed to understand two vital doctrines. The first was the doctrine of God's providential work among men. He believed the wicked suffer, whilst the righteous prosper. It is a principle that will govern the eternal duration of men, but it is not necessarily so during our life on earth. The Lord revealed a great contrast between the rich man and Lazarus in Luke 16. The rich man prospered in life, but suffered in eternity. Lazarus suffered in life but prospered in eternity.

God's providential dealings with men in this life differ. The wicked may prosper and not be in trouble as other men, whilst the righteous will often be found in the furnace of affliction.

When an ungodly man prospers in this life it must not be interpreted as an indication that that man has done something to merit such prosperity. It is a manifestation rather of the goodness of God. Likewise when the righteous suffer, it is permitted in the all wise and loving purpose of God, toward his people.

Herein we find the second doctrine Bildad confused. He said to Job if you were really upright God would awake for thee. In other words, if your life and works were true they would merit God's help, they would deserve divine aid. He was connecting divine favour to works and therefore confusing the doctrine of grace. He was making grace dependant on the works of man.

Behold the age old error we must avoid with all our heart. Grace can never be tied to works of human merit. John tells us in the first chapter of his gospel why we receive grace, it is "grace for grace" (v 16). It literally means we receive grace because, or on account of grace, not on account of what we are, or have done.

Why God Favours His People

Job 8:6 "If thou wert pure and upright; surely now he would awake for thee ..."

In the midst of all Job's suffering the charge of hypocrisy was laid upon him by his friends, firstly due to the great suffering that befell him and secondly because it seemed God had not arisen to his help. They inferred that these facts testified he was not an upright man.

Their insinuation betrayed their own ignorance of the gospel. The very heart of the gospel is the doctrine of imputation. Our sin was imputed to Christ who bore its punishment in our place. Christ's righteousness is imputed to our account and we enter into, receive and enjoy all the blessings that Christ earned by his obedience.

Bildad made the mistake of confusing imputed righteousness with inherent righteousness. He based God's favour and help upon the actual inherent righteousness of Job. If you were really pure in heart God would have helped you by now, but because he has not you are revealed as a hypocrite.

God's favour to his people is not conditional upon anything in us. God does not favour us only if we have a certain amount of faith, or holiness, or if we have prayed so much or performed a certain amount of good of works. God's favour is wholly unmerited and undeserved by us. His favour flows to us fully and freely, solely upon the merit of His dear Son.

Job was a child of God who excelled in godliness. But he was not sinless, within his heart there remained the remnant of corruption. God's favour was not bestowed upon him on account of his personal holiness, nor was it withdrawn because of his sin.

The ground of our acceptance by God remains eternally the righteousness of the Lord Jesus Christ. If we stray from this we will sink in despair. Grasp it and we will live in victory!

The Dos and Don'ts of Prayer

What a wonderful instruction our Lord gave to his disciples on prayer, through his sermon on the mount.

He gave them a warning on how not to pray.
Not to speak as the hypocrite, (v5). This word is taken from the 'theatre' and denotes someone who dresses up and plays the part of another; such seek to win the applause of another. The hypocrite prays in public places so others might praise them.

Neither do we pray as the heathen, (v7) who were known for their vain repetitions and babblings in prayer. After this manner the prophets of Baal entreated their god at Mount Carmel; (1Kings 18v26-28).

Our Lord gave a word of wisdom on how we ought to pray.
Notice that He took it for granted that the saints pray, "when thou prayest" (v5). As the natural man cannot live without breathing, so prayer is the air that the believer breathes; (Acts 9v11).

The place of prayer is called "thy closet" or inner chamber. True prayer is getting alone with the Lord, in the solitary place beyond the veil.

On occasions our Lord's closet was a mountain. He spent all night there, (Luke 6v12). May we too heed God's invitation to come up hither into his holy mount, and there like Moses speak to the Lord face to face, (Exodus 34v2). Oftimes our Saviour resorted to the Garden of Gethsemane, (John 18v1,2). Busy men, like Daniel should have set times of prayer.

There is also a need to shut the door on every distracting thought when we pray. Our hearts must be fixed on the Lord, by keeping silence before Him, (Isaiah 41v1). May every Christian have their place of prayer.

Our Heavenly Father

Matthew 6:9 "Our Father which art in Heaven."

Our blessed Lord has given us a pattern for prayer, (v9). As Moses was not to deviate from the pattern of the tabernacle, so we do not have liberty to turn aside from the model, as to how we ought to pray.

Although known as the Lord's Prayer, He never uttered it fully himself, as He was without sin and needed not forgiveness of any debt. By adhering to this pattern, we ask always according to God's will, (1 John 5v14,15).

The preface to the Lord's Prayer (v9) reveals that true prayer addresses Our Father in Heaven, what encouragement to know that the one we approach is not inaccessible light, but the one we call 'Abba Father'.

He is always accessible to every Christian.
That cannot be said of all others; to come into the Queen's presence you need royal permission. Yet with God we are accepted in the beloved, (Ephesians 1v6).

When we pray we approach an affectionate Father in Heaven.
He cares for you like no other, (1 Peter 5v7). Your interests are always on His heart, may we be anxious for nothing, (Philippians 4v6).

On a journey across the Atlantic, a Christian lady was not feeling too well, and she realised that an orange would help, so she asked the Lord for one. While she was sleeping on the deck a gentleman passed by, and placed two oranges on her lap. Later he asked if she had enjoyed the oranges, she replied 'yes' and expressed how good her Father was. The man looked astonished, "He cannot be alive?"

"Oh yes He is, and He loves me so much he brought me a double portion". He'll meet your every need too!

Our Holy Father

Matthew 6:9 "Hallowed be thy name."

As disciples of Jesus Christ we long that we may be divinely taught as to how we ought to pray (Luke 11v1). The petitions of the Lord's Prayer ought to be daily on our hearts.

The order of these petitions is important. The first three petitions have to do with our Lord's concerns regarding His name, kingdom and will. The last four petitions relate to our needs. So when you pray put God first, make sure He has the pre-eminence in what you ask for, (Colossians 1v18).

This request asks that God's name might be set apart from every other name. It is not a common name but a sacred name. "Holy and reverend is Thy name" (Psalm 111v9).

From 300BC the Jewish race refused to speak any more Jehovah's name. They did not want to profane his holy name; the scribe handled that name carefully. He bathed before he would translate that name and the quill was never used again to write a lesser name. Common expressions like "for goodness sake" or "gosh" actually profane the Lord's name. Remember His name is precious as ointment that is poured forth, (Song of Solomon 1v3).

God's name also reveals His true character, who He is. At creation He made himself known as Elohim (Genesis 1v2). Later to Abraham He appeared as El Shaddai, the almighty God (Genesis 17v1). Now He has made Himself known as Jehovah, the unchanging One.

God's name being set apart must be our main concern. We want to see Him magnified and made great among all nations, (Psalm 34v3).

The Prayer for Divine Progress

Matthew 6:10 "Thy kingdom come."

In this second petition we ask that Christ's Kingdom might be established. Every King has a kingdom; there is a twofold aspect that we pray with regard to His kingdom.

That the Kingdom of Grace might come
We beseech God to set up His kingdom in men's hearts, where He reigns as King of their lives. This is accomplished when the mighty gospel of Christ opens the sinner's heart (Acts 16v14). Through the new birth the individual then enters into the kingdom of God's dear Son, (Colossians 1v13). At the time of Christ's public ministry many looked for this kingdom to be established outwardly (in Israel itself), but the Lord revealed that His kingdom dwells within a man, (Luke 17v2).

That the Kingdom of Glory might come
When this happens, the earth is made his footstool (Psalm 110v1). After ascending on high, our Lord was highly exalted by His Father and received the Kingdom of Heaven. There the Lamb has all the glory in Emmanuel's land. After our Lord returns again to this earth, it will be filled with His glory (Psalm72v19). Our Lord will sit on David's throne and reign forever and ever.

The Puritans called this great truth, 'the eschatology of victory'. What an encouragement to every saint, to know that every enemy will be placed under Jesus' feet. Satan to Jesus must bow. May this motivate us to do greater exploits for Him, as through Christ we know a life of overcoming.

Finally, to enter into the Kingdom of Glory one must first enter the Kingdom of Grace. For a worshipper to enter into the Temple of Honour at Athens, they first had to pass through the House of Virtue. There is no other divinely appointed way to enter into God's Kingdom (John 3v5).

The Prayer for Divine Provision

Matthew 6:11 "Give us this day our daily bread."

The fourth petition is a confident request that the Lord would supply our temporal needs, in particular regarding food. The English puritan Thomas Watson said that God's tree of mercy, which is laden with many fruits; cannot drop them until it is shaken by the hand in prayer. We must ask in order to receive.

We ought to pray as Agur did "feed me with food convenient for me" (Proverbs 30v8). He looked to the Lord for his daily allowance and content with that. Truly "Godliness with contentment is great gain" (1 Timothy 6v6).

Are we not encouraged to know that the Lord is already acquainted with our need even before we ask for it. "Your Heavenly Father knoweth that ye have need of all these things" (Ch 6v32).

The promise of our daily bread
All who seek first God's kingdom are to be anxious for nothing, (6v33). God will take care of their needs as they see to his concerns. While the Israelites marched through a great wilderness under Moses leadership, the Lord graciously furnished a table for them in the wilderness. Manna covered the earth every evening. Even His enemies received their portion, instead of spreading a net for their feet; He spread a table for their physical nourishment.

The perpetuality of our daily bread
It was faithfully given every day of the journey from Egypt to Canaan. Once they entered into the land of promise, the Israelites ate the corn of the land, (Joshua 5v11). The righteous will never beg for bread, (Psalm 37v25,26).

The praise for our daily bread
Every meal we partake of should be received with thanksgiving, always be sure to give grace, (1 Timothy 4 v3-5).

The Prayer for Divine Pardon

Matthew 6:12 "and forgive us our debts"

There is an important link between the 4th and 5th petition, conveyed by the conjunction 'and'. Christ Jesus teaches that temporal blessings will profit a man nothing unless they experience God's mercy. This is the only petition that our Lord comments on afterwards, (6v14-15).

The confession that we require forgiveness
Not to confess is to cover our sin thereby we do not prosper (Proverbs 28v13). Let us acknowledge that like David we sin against the Lord and have done evil in His sight, (Psalm 51v4).

Praise the Lord our sin may be pardoned as Christ has made a full compensation for them at Calvary. A fountain for sin has been opened in the house of David, (Zechariah 13v1). God's pardon is great as he is abundant in forgiveness (Isaiah 55v7).

The character of this remarkable forgiveness
To be forgiven implies that God has passed by our transgressions, (Micah 7v18). Our slate has been wiped clean. Two red lines have been drawn across our account declaring, "It has been paid in full by Jesus blood". All who have been forgiven have their sins removed from them and cast into the depths of the sea, (Micah 7v19).

The condition to receiving forgiveness (6v14)
It is easier to pray to God to forgive us, than it is for us to forgive others who have offended us. Yet we are to forgive seventy times seven, (Matthew 18v22). How blessed are the merciful for they shall obtain mercy (Matthew 5v7).

The Prayer for Divine Protection

Matthew 6:13 "deliver us from evil."

Christians are not of this world but are citizens of Heaven. It is God's will for them to remain in this world, (John 17v15). To abide here is presently more needful for you child of God. What an influence we have in the world, we save others from the corruption of sin.

In this world we are exposed to temptation
God's people are the lily abiding among thorns (Song of Solomon 2v2), the sheep among ravening wolves (Matthew 10v16).

There are evils we must resist. The Devil as a roaring lion seeks to devour every saint, (1 Peter 5v8). We must resist the devil and he will flee.

The present world must not be loved (1 John 2v15), remember Demas (2 Timothy 4v10). Our flesh must be crucified daily. Martin Luther feared his heart more than the pope or his cardinals. May we make no provision for the flesh (Romans 13v14).

In this world we expect temptation
Our adversary is the god of this world and we are passing through hostile territory, "In this world ye shall have tribulation" (John 16v33). As the world hated Christ, so they will hate his disciples (John 17v14). We must ask the Lord to enable us to endure temptation, do not live as a hermit in a place of seclusion, rather know God's grace to patiently endure the trial of our faith.

In this world we are equipped for temptation
The Holy Scriptures cleanse our way and keep our hearts from sin. Our Great High Priest intercedes in Heaven for us, causing our faith not to fail when Satan sifts us as wheat (Luke 22v31-32). How thankful we are to be kept by God's mighty power.

A Timely Reminder

"The book of the generations of Adam" marks the second main division of Genesis, which finishes at the Flood (the first is "the generations of the heavens and the earth" – Genesis 2:4).

Verses 1 and 2 re-affirm God's direct creation of Adam and Eve. This was first enunciated in Genesis 1:26, 27, then in Genesis 2:7, 20-22.

Their distinction is also noted, "Male and female created He them"; their benediction, "And blessed them"; and their appellation, "And called their name Adam." Both had a common origin. Adam was made from the dust of the ground and Eve was "taken out of man" (Genesis 2:23).

These things are repeated here because God wants us to know how seriously He takes them, and because we too easily forget them.
We need to remind ourselves every day that we owe our life to God "in whose hand our breath is" (Daniel 5:23). Forgetfulness can be fatal. Belshazzar, king of Babylon, forgot and Daniel told him "God has numbered your kingdom and finished it" (Daniel 5:26).

The distinction of the sexes and God's blessing the union of male and female must also be constantly borne in mind in an age when anything goes.
It comes in this chapter before the illustrations of human mortality and the implication of a coming judgment for man's sin. "Death passed upon all men for that all men sinned." So no matter how used mankind is to his own depravity, it will never justify his corruption of God's way and God's standards. He has said, "Marriage is honourable in all... adulterers God will judge" (Hebrews 13:4).

Like Father like Son

The likeness and image of Adam fixed on Seth was not the Divine image in which he himself had been created.
"Image" is something spiritual, and God's image has to do with "knowledge" (Colossians 3:10) which is the right understanding of spiritual things, and "righteousness and holiness" (Ephesians 4:24), a perfect moral condition. But man forfeited these by the Fall, and they are only renewed in regeneration.

The image of Adam is fixed on all men.
It means that by nature they are without proper apprehension of spiritual things. That is why they fail to grasp saving truth. Nicodemus is an example. He was religious but thought that to be born again meant entering a second time into his mother's womb!

It means that by nature men do not stand in a right relationship with God, and that this affects their behaviour toward others. When Adam was righteous and holy before God he enjoyed fellowship with him and was in harmony with the world. When he sinned he ran from God and used his wife as an excuse for his sin (Genesis 3:12).

This emphasises our need of a thorough conversion.
That is through Jesus, who, as God, was sinless, and whose human nature was supernaturally conceived and therefore impeccable (Matthew 1:20). Only He can make us "new creatures". Having saved us He begins to conform us to His image (2 Corinthians 3:18), and one day we will be sinless too. What a privilege! What a Saviour! What a cause for praise!

Lessons from Longevity

There are two main features in this chronology -

First, the longevity of Adam and his descendants, whose average age was 912.
That these are literal years may be argued on the ground that the patriarchs must have had vigorous constitutions - the world was not ravaged by the diseases it is today. Diet too must have had something to do with the longevity of the patriarchs.

But the strongest argument is that it was in keeping with the Divine purpose. Every man mentioned here had sons and daughters. That means at least four children each. When so many lived for so long and their lives overlapped, generations would not die out quickly and time would therefore be sufficient to "multiply" and fill the earth.

The longevity of the patriarchs also helped to preserve a knowledge of God. All except Noah were born before Adam died. So they would have heard from him about creation, the Fall, the promise of a Deliverer (Genesis 3:15).

Second, God keeps before us here the transient nature of our life.
God numbers our days before life begins (Acts 17:26; Job 14:5), and reckons them by days (V.8). Life is transient also because of sin and the words, "And he died," show God's faithfulness to His threat – "Dust thou art and unto dust shalt thou return."

So the longest life will end. But what good will a long life do you if you are not converted? The impenitent will have all eternity to rue every year, indeed every day, wasted in sin. Salvation is more important than a long life. "Thy lovingkindness is better than life" (Psalm 63:3).

Enoch : The Commencement of his Walk with God

His father was unknown, except by name and age.
His name occurs only nine times in Scripture. He lived only half the years of his contemporaries. His Old Testament biography is covered in four verses. Still, Enoch the son of Jared had an outstanding testimony and his godliness is an example to believers in all ages.

However, for the first sixty-five years of his life he lived without God.
He conducted himself without any sense of his need. Only after his son was born he began to walk with God. Some only begin to think about God when they settle down and have a family. But far better to walk with God from early years, so that your life is full, and before responsibilities become so heavy you find it impossible to think of anything else.

When his son was born God showed Enoch that the world was going to be destroyed.
He named him "Methuselah", which means "after he is dead it shall come" – i.e. the Flood. He would not live to see it, but if he died he knew he would meet his Maker unprepared, and so he called on God for pardon. So the revelation of coming judgment is reason to seek mercy. We are told to "flee from the wrath to come."

For the sake of the younger generation, and for the sake of our children, we must walk with God.
A good example may lead them to the Saviour. The failure to walk with God may result in their being lost for ever.

Enoch : The Characteristics of his Walk with God

Walking with God means companying with God.
He is near to His people, but they are to keep near to Him too. So here it is not said that "God walked with Enoch" but that "Enoch walked with God." He chose to keep in His company and be in constant communion with Him.

Walking with God means concord with God.
Amos 3:3, "Can two walk together except thee be agreed?" Enoch agreed with God's view of him as a sinner ("confession", 1 John 1:9, means "to say the same thing"). Enoch agreed with God's revelation of Himself. He did not argue with it, as rebels do (Luke 16:30), but preached it as it was (Jude V.14).

Walking with God means confidence in God.
Who would keep company with someone they didn't trust? Enoch trusted God (Hebrews 11:5,6).

Walking with God means constancy with God.
The Hebrew is, "Enoch walked to and fro with God." Everywhere he went he took the Lord with him. After other sons and daughters were born he walked with God while carrying out his domestic business.

Walking with God means conformity to God.
It is said that when someone is in another's company for a long time they become like that person. They learn his ways (Proverbs 13:20, 22:25). Jesus said, "Come unto me...take my yoke upon thee and learn of me..." (Matthews 11:28-30).

Walking with God is what He requires. It is the Christian's duty.
"What doth the Lord require of thee, but to do justly, and to love mercy, and to walk humbly with thy God?" (Micah 6:8).

Enoch : The Consummation of his Walk with God

"Enoch was not" does not mean that he was annihilated.

"God took him" implies that he was taken somewhere. Hebrews 11:5 says he was "translated" i.e. carried from one place to the next. There was another man who God took without his dying – Elijah. He went up into Heaven in a whirlwind. So it is clear that that is where Enoch was taken. Millions of believers will go to Heaven without dying (1 Thessalonians 4:17).

As well as showing us where he was taken, the Bible shows us why he was taken.

He was taken because God was pleased with him (Hebrews 11:5). Like him, you can only have the testimony of a believer if you are a believer. Implied is the fact that God does not take unbelievers to Heaven.

He was missed when he was taken.

Men looked for him but he couldn't be found (Hebrews 11:5). He was taken from his sons and daughters and they missed him. I wonder how Methuselah must have felt? In the midst of sorrow he must have rejoiced that his father had gone to Heaven, and also been grateful, and humbled by the fact that he had been the means God used to awaken Enoch to his need of salvation. If you have been used by God to point a loved one to Christ, give Him the praise!

But then there is this other question. When you are gone will you be missed? Enoch's family missed the man who had walked with God. They must have appreciated his testimony. Will your family miss you for your testimony when God takes you, Christian?

The Goodness of God

The closing words of this chapter present us with wonderful illustrations of the goodness of God.
There is His goodness in longsuffering. As long as Methuselah lived God stayed His hand of judgment from the world and gave men space to repent. According to Bible chronology the Flood was sent the year he died.

The goodness of God is seen in His grace toward Methuselah's family.
His son Lamech named his son "Noah" in hope of the change that would come to the world through him as God's instrument. He spoke in faith. Noah did bring comfort. His building of the Ark proved that God had provided a way of escape. Because of his sacrifice in the new world God said He wouldn't curse the ground any more (Genesis 8:21). Lamech's faith was by the word of God (Romans 10:17). God told him about his son's future, just as He revealed to Moses' parents that he would be a deliverer (Hebrews 11:23). Methuselah's grandson was also a believer, for later we read that "Noah walked with God" (Genesis 6:9).

Salvation does not run in the blood, but it can run in families by the grace of God.
Paul said about Timothy, "When I call to remembrance the unfeigned faith that is in thee, which dwelt first in thy grandmother Lois and thy mother Eunice; and I am persuaded that in thee also" (2 Timothy 1:5). Many believing children owe their salvation, under God, to a grandmother, mother or father, and should thank the Lord. Parents can also rejoice when their witness is made effectual to the conversion of their children.